How To Be
OUTRAGEOUSLY
Successful
with the
Opposite Sex

How To Solve Every Problem You've Ever Had...
Meeting, Dating or Marrying
the Man or Woman of Your Dreams

---

by

Paul Hartunian

Published by

❖ **Ultimate Secrets**

Box 43033
Upper Montclair, NJ 07043

Published by
◆ **Ultimate Secrets**
Box 43033
Upper Montclair, NJ 07043
201-857-6283

First Printing . . . . *February, 1991*
Second Printing, Revised . . . . *May, 1991*
Third Printing, Revised . . *September, 1991*

ISBN 0-939038-02-1

Library of Congress Catalogue #91-90806

Library of Congress Cataloging-in-Publication Data

Hartunian, Paul.
    How to be outrageously successful with the opposite sex : how to solve every problem you've ever had - meeting, dating, or marrying the man or woman of your dreams / by Paul Hartunian.
        p.   cm.
    ISBN 0-939038-02-1 : $19.95
    1. Dating (Social customs) 2. Interpersonal relations. 3. Single persons--United States. I. Title.
HQ801.H352   1991
646.7'7--dc20   91-90806
                                                                              CIP

Designed by Carl Galletti

DEDICATION

This book is dedicated to people who see life as a series of great opportunities, not disabling problems; people who truly understand the meaning of "carpe diem" - seize the day; people who are the thinkers and doers of the world. I give you all a standing ovation.

THANKS!

Dr. Rob Gilbert has been a great sounding board for my ideas for the past 10 years. His help with this book was immeasurable. His friendship is one of my most valued possessions. You'll read more about him later in this book. You'll also find a special phone number for Dr. Gilbert. Call it! I guarantee it will be one of the best calls you'll ever make.

Marybeth Ray has been one of my most trusted, respected and beloved friends for about 20 years. While she was on a Caribbean cruise, she spent hours reviewing this book and coming up with suggestions. My thanks and love go to her along with the hope that we have at least another 20 years of friendship to look forward to.

Milt Horowitz, a relative newcomer to my circle of friends but appreciated just as much, was able to take a computer disk full of vital information and translate it into a language I can read - English. Without that information, I would have suffered a serious setback in getting this book published. Thanks, Milt!

Jeffrey Lant has written several books - books that have changed my life. As I'm fond of saying: "If I lost everything I had except for Jeffrey's books, I'd use the books to get everything back within a year." Thank you, my friend.

Josh Rasp is the best friend a guy could want to have...a lot of fun and a real, true pal. Josh was the inspiration for a part of this book. My thanks go to you too, my friend.

Carl Galletti is a whiz! It's that simple. He designed this book and has had an incredibly steady flow of great ideas for me. He's a brilliant copywriter and a marketing genius. If you should ever meet Carl, don't let him get away. With his talents and abilities, he'll be able to help you make some major advances in your life.

TABLE OF CONTENTS

SECTION 3 - The Secrets

—————————————————

INTRODUCTION

This book was designed to help you get everything you've dreamed about when it comes to the opposite sex - whether you are male or female. Your objective can be success with one member of the opposite sex - a complete, all encompassing, passionate relationship with that one person of your dreams.

Or, you may want to be surrounded by an entire flock of members of the opposite sex. That's your decision. It's up to you. You are the only person who can decide what "Outrageous Success With the Opposite Sex" means. So, when I talk about "Outrageous Success", I'm talking about how you have defined it. Not someone else's definition. This book will help you accomplish your objective -

IF IT'S WHAT YOU REALLY WANT!

If you're not serious, this book will just be entertaining reading. If you're serious and you're willing to take action, success is right around the corner. I have the roadmap. You're the driver. We'll make the journey together.

Let's get started!

Let me ask you a question. Why aren't people successful with the opposite sex? I'm convinced that there is only one reason.

THEY DON'T TRY!

They don't go for it!

Oh, they may put up a front.

They go to dances. They join a dating service. Maybe they answer or place a personal ad. But this is, indeed, just a front. The approaches I just mentioned are usually done in a rote, robot-like fashion. They're done with the anticipation of failure. Then, when failure inevitably comes, it's no surprise. Dance after dance. Party after party. Failure after failure.

In fact, to some it appears hopeless. That's when you start hearing "It's impossible to meet a normal woman." Or "All men are creeps." For them, the war may be over. They have surrendered.

But if you know that the picture can be much brighter, you're about to be rescued. You <u>know</u> it's not hopeless. You may just not be sure how to make it hopeful. <u>Keep</u> reading. The battle is coming to an end...and you're going to be the winner!

<u>WHAT YOU'LL FIND IN THIS BOOK</u>

Following this introduction there are 33 chapters.

The first section is called "The Methods". This section is packed with ingenious, exciting, successful methods of meeting the opposite sex. These methods have already been used and tested. They work. They're waiting <u>for</u> <u>you</u> to put them into action. There are ideas that will be just perfect for you. All the techniques work - if you work them!

The second section is called "The Mistakes". In this section you'll learn about the 10 mistakes most people make in meeting, winning and dating the opposite sex. You'll learn exactly what the mistakes are and how to avoid them. You'll learn why they are mistakes and why you shouldn't fall into their traps. You'll learn precisely how not to succumb to them. You'll also find out which <u>one</u> of these 10 mistakes is the biigest!

The next section is "The Secrets". This is my favorite section. In this part of the book I reveal to you, for the first time ever, <u>the greatest secrets</u> to success with the opposite sex. These secrets will propel you to new heights of success.

FAIR WARNING!!! Before you read this section, be prepared! You'll experience greater, quicker success than you've ever experienced in all the years of your life. This success may come so quickly and so easily that you'll be amazed. You'll get such a rush of success that you might be unprepared. You'll be so successful that you'll be disoriented & temporarily unable to decide which road to take - unless you are prepared. Unless you are ready to handle it.

Finally, there's the last section - "The Summary". Here we put everything we've learned into a nice little package. A package that'll be my gift to you - certainly a gift you won't want to return the next day.

By the time you get to the summary you'll be overflowing with new, creative, exciting ideas that you'll be able to instantly put into action to meet the man or woman - or men or women - that have filled your fantasies. Never again will you be at a loss for ways to find those special men or women. The only time you'll be alone on a weekend is when you want to take a breather from all the activity.

No more ego-bashing bars. Or dream-crushing blind dates. No more set ups. No creeps, weenies or losers. You'll win back control of your social life. You won't be at the mercy of others.

HOW TO GET THE MOST OUT OF THIS BOOK

This manual is packed full of ideas - not just a few ideas or a dozen ideas. It's overflowing with ideas. Great ideas. Ideas that have worked - and are working. Your only problem will be how to sort through them all.

Read this book with a red pen in hand. As you read, mark up this book. Underline good thoughts. Put stars next to ideas that you can put to use in your own life.

Put one star next to ideas that you find mildly interesting. These are ideas that may take more courage than you have now. Or ideas that you'll have to change a bit before you put them into acton.

Put two stars next to ideas that are of fairly strong interest. These are ideas that you can put right into action and have success.

Then there are the three star ideas.

These are the ones that make you squirm in your seat; make your heart beat fast; make your eyes open wide and your pupils dilate. These are the ideas that hit home so hard that you just know they're going to work. You're positive. You know the battle is over. You know that you and the new person that's about to come into your life have won! These are the ideas that are so perfect for you and that get you so excited you might not have time to put three stars next to them. You'll be too busy putting them into action. These are the answers you've been looking for.

WHO AM I AND WHAT MAKES ME
QUALIFIED TO WRITE THIS BOOK?

You know my name. Now the "qualifications". I always laugh when people ask me how I'm qualified to speak & write on this subject. What are they looking for? A degree in dating. A license to practice successful encounters with women?

So, what <u>does</u> qualify me (just in case you <u>do</u> want to know). The answer is simple.

Results!

That's it.

Results.

I've been fortunate enough to be involved with some of the greatest women in the world. Women who have charmed me with their beauty, brains, wit and accomplishments. Women who have added new joy to my life. Women who have burned magnificent, indelible memories into my mind. Women whose faces will be with me until I close my eyes for the last time.

What's brought me this great success? Some special talent? Great wealth? Irresistible power? Chisled features and the body of a Greek God?

Hardly.

Very simply, my success has come because I've learned to overcome fear. I'm not afraid to go after what I want. Not afraid to seek out and try new ideas. Not afraid to enjoy every moment and molecule of a magnificent woman.

THE LAST THING YOU'LL READ BEFORE
YOUR WHOLE LIFE CHANGES

So far, I've been talking about success with women. Trust me, my friend, I only speak of success with women because I am a man. This book is meant for <u>women</u> as well as men. This manual is full of exciting ideas that women can use to be outrageously successful with the opposite sex.

It makes absolutely no difference whether you're male or female. This book is <u>for you</u>. The only thing that makes a difference is your desire to get what you want. If you have a burning desire to be successful with the opposite sex, I can virtually guarantee that that is exactly what you'll have when you and I have finished.

If your desire is less than burning, I'll help you fan the flames of desire and then set you on your way. You, too, will be successful, I assure you.

If, though, you're one of the seriously wounded soldiers I spoke of earlier, we may have a problem. If bitterness, anger and suspicion have taken you over, you'll have to let go of that first. If you greeted this introduction with snide remarks, sharp criticism and mountains of doubt, success may not be staring you in the face. If, on the other hand, you can put those feelings aside, just for a while, I promise to work with you until you succeed. Only you can decide your fate. But, I can help.

Turn this page with a real sense of excitement. The next several hours we'll spend together will be very exciting.

You've bought a book. You've also bought a friend, advisor & confidant. If I can be of help to you, don't hesitate to call on me. Not to whine or moan. Not to tell me how terrible life is. I have absolutely no tolerance for that.

But, I'm here to share your joys and successes. I'm here to answer questions for you on your way to ecstasy. I'm here to give you those words of support you may need when you feel that little devil, fear, but you want to do it anyway.

SPECIAL NOTE

At the end of many of these chapters, you'll find information about various products and services for single men and women -- magazines & newspapers, books, a dating service, etc.

I've looked into each and every one of these and feel that they are of good quality and high value. I want to pass this information on to you as an extra bonus. If you're like most of us, you're concerned about getting the most for your money. I can assure you that each of these products or services will give you excellent value at a great price. Buy them with confidence.

OK. It's time to get to work on changing your love life...<u>forever</u>!

Chapter 1

YOUR BIGGEST ENEMY - FEAR

It's everyone's dream - being "Outrageously Successful With the Opposite Sex". Being surrounded by gorgeous men or women...the center of romantic and sexual attention. But it's all fantasy.

I'm not really sure where things went wrong. It seems so simple.

Boy meets girl.

Boy romances girl.

Boy and girl live happily ever after. It just doesn't seem that being single should be so difficult. Finding and meeting people that bring you to the heights of ecstacy shouldn't be an ordeal of fire.

Well then why is it?

The answer is simple.

It's fear.

That's it.

Plain and simple.

Fear.

So why isn't this book about how to conquer fear? Because there are two ways to conquer a mountain - you can climb it or you can walk around it. Fear has become the biggest mountain known to man. We're not going to learn to climb it in just one book - lots of people have tried. It doesn't work. So, let's walk around it for now. The results will be the same. We'll be on the other side of the mountain. We just took a different route.

I'll show you the path around the mountain. In fact, I'll show you lots of paths around this mountain. You choose the one - or the ones - you'd like to take.

But before we start this trip, I have to get back to fear. Maybe, just maybe, by reading these few pages, some of you will be able to climb the mountain and meet us on the other side a lot sooner.

Irrational fear is not normal. You weren't born with it. It's not part of your "basic equipment". It's not useful. In fact, it's harmful. Notice I said irrational fear. That's almost all fear.

Now, of course, some fear is normal - the fear of imminent, real danger, such as an oncoming car, a collapsing wall, a fire in your home. It's real. It can cause very real problems if not dealt with. If we don't have this type of fear - or awareness - we have a different problem.

But those other fears - the fear of not being good enough, not looking good enough, not being smart enough...you made them up. OK, I'll agree that you probably had a lot of help making them up. Television has told you how lethal your feet, breath & underarms are. Your boss has told you how lazy you are. When you were in school, the other kids made sure that you were always kept aware of every little fault you had. You know, your parents may even have contributed to this situation - banish the thought!

The world hasn't helped you -- but you're responsible too. You bought it! You bought everything they told you about yourself. And you know what's even more curious? Most people only buy the bad things: the things people tell them are "wrong" with them. For some reason, they don't buy the good news - the things that are "right" with them.

So, you bought it.

You could have returned it! You could have said "This is not for me. I'm just fine. I'm returning these negative thoughts to you, world. I don't want them."

OK, so you bought it and kept it for a while. Most of us did. You don't have to keep it forever! It's not like a tattoo. It's more like pantyhose. When it wears out, throw it out. Don't keep it around. It's useless. In fact, it's less than useless. It's a problem.

Well, not everyone buys it. Most of us do, but not everyone.

In my years as a speaker and author, I've had the opportunity to ask hundreds of people what made them successful. I don't just mean successful with the opposite sex. I mean successful in life. I wanted just a few words they lived by. A quote. Or a saying. Whatever. I've asked Presidents, Supreme Court Justices, athletes, entertainers, Nobel Prize winners. But the best response came from Bette Davis.

She gave me an answer that hit the bullseye for me. It's just four words.

Four words that make up one of the greatest secrets of the universe.

Four words that no one can doubt.

Four words that can make you "Outrageously Successful With the Opposite Sex" or outrageously successful with anything else you could ever want.

What are they?

Simple.

"NO GUTS, NO GLORY"

It says it all. It's the greatest secret of the universe. It's true. If you have the guts, you get the glory. It's as simple as that. If you have no guts, you get no glory...and you shouldn't expect it...and you shouldn't complain that "it's not fair". Because the people with the guts are getting the glory...and they deserve it.

You know, I have this image of what happens when you die. God calls you over and says "Have a seat. I just want to ask you one question. Where did all this fear come from? I didn't give it to you. Oh sure, I made you afraid of things that could cause you danger. But I didn't make you afraid of everything you were afraid of!"

Remember that person you met on October 27, 1991? The one that you couldn't stop staring at? The one that made your heart beat so fast? I put that person there for you. Why didn't you say something... or do something? You let those fears you made up run your life. And I've got to tell you, you passed up a lot of great opportunities."

OK. So I just beat you up a little bit. What a way to start a book! Actually, I'm really a nice guy. I just wanted to get the juices flowing a bit.

Come on. I have a whole book full of great ideas for you. We'll do it together. Let's go get the glory!!

The Florida Singles

Entertainer

The leading singles paper in Florida

• Circulation of 0ver 50,000 through out Florida & South Georgia
• FREE Photo with your personal ad
•900 phone number for those who don't like to write letters
•Low personal ad fee
•Excellent response
• Subscription and free circulation

Get a <u>FREE</u> personal ad up to 40 words with your paid subscription
plus
A FREE photo

Subscription price:
6 months ( ) $10
1 year (') $18

Mailing Address:
Florida Singles Entertainer
P.O. Box 76085
Ocala, Florida 32676
904-854-1008

Chapter 2

THE FIRST STEP

For the best part of two years, I tracked down information on the "problems" of being single. Actually, I wanted to find out how other people are happily surrounding themselves with other enjoyable singles.

My search started by simply talking to single people around the country and in a few other countries. I wanted to hear their complaints -- I got a lot of those. But I also wanted to hear how they were solving the problem.

After the lengthy complaints of "no good men" and "no good women" being available, I started to hear solutions. But I wasn't happy. The solutions I was hearing were not solutions at all. They were merely band-aids on amputations. People were pouring out long complaints about the availability of suitable singles, but they were trying to solve the problem by standing in singles bars...that's it. Nothing else. In fact, the overwhelming majority of people I spoke to were using very typical methods of meeting other singles...and no other methods at all. They were essentially using bars, dating services, dances and parties.

Let me say clearly and up front that I do not have a problem with bars, dating services and so on - as long as they are not the only method you use to meet people. They are just fine if they are each a small part of your singles arsenal. Used exclusively, though, this arsenal will explode in your face.

The techniques I'll be describing in the rest of this book are ingenious. They're fun. Most importantly, they work!

I'll give you dozens of great ideas you can use to meet other singles...including the "man or woman of your dreams".

The bottom line, though, is that all I can do in this book is tell you what works. You have to do it. This will be entirely your choice. You can be totally convinced that these methods work. But, unless you take some action, nothing will happen.

This book can occupy just another spot on your shelf. Or, it can be the manual that brings you to ecstacy. Obviously, I want it to be your ecstacy manual.

When I'm on one of your local radio or TV talk shows, I want you to call in and tell me about how you are deleriously happy. And I'll want to talk to your newly found "better half" too.

But you know what I don't want you to do? I don't want you to call to tell me that the book doesn't work. I know that's not true. I have the evidence. It works. And it works well!

The people who came up with these ideas are brilliant. They knew that there was no sense in going into the arena with everyone else and doing battle. They were willing to stand outside and let the people inside battle it out. They went their own way...along a less crowded road...with less competition...and fewer problems...and more success. They're in ecstacy!

With some lack of modesty, I've got to tell you that a number of these ideas are mine. Aside from my teenage years - when we were all a bit nuts - I've never had much trouble with women. I love them. They're sheer delights. Reasons to be alive and thankful for life. So, when I would hear the seemingly unending complaints, I was surprised to say the least. This book and the research that went into it were a quest to find out if I've just been lucky or if there were lots of other people having success.

I breathed a sigh of relief when I found lots of other people sharing my success. Women having great success with men. Men having great success with women.

Take my word for it. There are lots of people having success with the opposite sex. We want you to join us.

The methods, mistakes, morals and motivations in this book are going to make the difference for you.

Let's get going.

What do you have to lose?

SECTION 1

THE METHODS

Chapter 3

THE PEOPLE BEHIND THE IDEAS

It's happened to all of us. We are surrounded by couples who must have just come out of the centerfold of "Cute Couple" magazine. They're all smiles and so much in love. If we happen to be in the same situation at the time, we smile with that knowing look. We're there too.

If we aren't in the same situation, though, watch out! That little creature in our minds starts to really beat us up.

Why aren't we in that type of relationship?

Where are all the good people?

And then there's the biggie...what's wrong with me? Well, there's nothing at all wrong with you. You just were given the wrong directions.

Let's say you stopped at a gas station on the way to a meeting in a strange town. You're lost. You ask for directions. The attendant tells you to travel down the road you're on for 25 miles, turn right, go another 6 miles and you'll be there. You soon find out that his directions were wrong. The only place you got was 31 miles further out of your way. Was that your fault? Of course not!!! You depended on a person you thought was an authority. You were simply misled. You acted on bad information.

Well, when we want to meet someone of the opposite sex, we're often in the same boat. We get information from our parents, who may have very different values than ours. We pay attention to customs...things that have been done for centuries, whether they're right or not. We listen to that little devil inside us that says "Don't do that", "That's silly", "You might fail" and other "helpful" advice.

If there's one force in our lives we should probably always ignore, it's that little voice in our heads. If you're saying to yourself, "There's no little voice in my head", that's the little voice I'm talking about! Generally, that little voice is not on your side. It's not working for you, only against you.

So what do we do? That's what I wanted to know. So, I searched around the country to find people who were having great success with their social lives. People who were not depending on the bars to provide their thrills. People who had come up with answers.

I found them.

In fact, I found lots of them.

First, let me assure you that each of these people is quite average in every way. If their photos were mixed into a group of 100 other photos, they wouldn't stand out as being especially attractive. In fact, they range from somewhat unattractive to slightly above average. To look at them, you wouldn't see any special qualities. They didn't have particularly bubbly personalities, although each one had a pleasant personality. Their dress was nice, but nothing special.

Well, then, what was it that made these people unusual? What do they have that most others do not?

The answer is imagination.

Although they didn't all say it in this way, they all indicated the same feeling. They all knew that they were simply members of a very large group, that group being single people looking for other singles. Each one of them knew that if they wanted to enjoy outrageous success with the opposite sex, they would have to stand out in some way.

Actually, they saw their job as simple. Just come up with one way to stand out and success is almost guaranteed. Oh yes, they had one other thing...the desire to put their ideas into action. They weren't afraid to take action. Actually, they looked forward to it, because they were not happy with the situation they had. They each had had enough of the endless competition from other singles.

Their ages, incomes, physical proportions and educations varied pretty substantially. The only thing they did share, and the only thing that seemed to make a difference, was the ability to ignore the little negative voice and let their imaginations go. They had a problem and they were determined to solve it. And solve it they did.

Were they nervous? Sure, sometimes. But the feeling of excitement was greater than the feeling of nervousness. And oh, those rewards. They clearly saw the rewards right in front of them. All they had to do was get into action.

Let me say right now that I'll be giving you lots of terrific ideas you can use to become outrageously successful with the opposite sex. You can use them all, if you want. I doubt you'll want to do that, though. Not all of these ideas will be for everybody. You may find lots of ideas you can use. You may only find a few. But, remember,

YOU ONLY NEED ONE GOOD IDEA AND YOUR LIFE COULD BE CHANGED!

Don't immediately rule out any idea. I can't tell you how many times people thought an idea was crazy. As they thought about it, though, the crazy idea became a clever idea. Then the clever idea became a great idea. Then the great idea became an idea that worked.

Some of the ideas in this book can be used by very shy people. Others take a little courage. Some are just for men. Some are just for women. Most are for both. Some cost money. Most don't. All of them are fun. Some will even give you belly laughs, which will make them a whole lot easier to try.

None of these ideas are engraved in granite. I present them to you the way they were presented to me. If you have a new slant to an idea, try it! In fact, if you have a new slant or an entirely new idea, let me know. You'll be mentioned in the next edition of "How to Be Outrageously Successful With the Opposite Sex"...and that certainly couldn't hurt your social life! In fact, let's make this my first idea for you. Come up with a new idea or new slant and send it to me at

❖ Ultimate Secrets
Box 43033
Upper Montclair, NJ 07043.

When the next edition of this book comes out I'll be sure to put the spotlight squarely on you. You can take it from there.

What do you have to lose?

Chapter 4

COOKING FOR THE SINGLE MALE??!!??

I'll never know why certain people have problems meeting the person of their dreams.

You know the kind I'm talking about. They look great, have personalities that just about knock you out, they have interesting jobs and they have the skill to hold a conversation with a caveman.

Nevertheless, I can't tell you how many of these people I run across. In fact, we've all heard about the gorgeous woman who sits home on a Saturday night because no one has the courage to ask her out. And to look at the other side of the story, she probably hasn't done much to improve the situation.

I was like most of you. I thought it was a bunch of nonsense. I had dreams of the thrilling lives these women were living. Well, I found lots of gorgeous women who knew all about Saturdays at home. There were lots of gorgeous men who were not exactly thrilled with their social lives, either.

So, maybe it's fitting that this first method is about a friend of mine, Lori, who certainly fits into this category. Lori has just about got it all...looks, personality, brains, job. The only thing she did not have was an exciting, enjoyable relationship.

I didn't understand it, but it was true.

Lori and I spent lots of time talking about her situation. She told me about the men she would meet. She would also tell me about the men she wouldn't meet! Lori is very typical in one way. She thinks that the man should make the first move. In fact, she has a real battle about just that thought. She is a "Today Woman". She knows that there is absolutely nothing wrong with a woman making the first move, but she just can't do it. I'm sure there are a lot of reasons for this -- family, religion, etc. -- but the bottom line is that she has convinced herself that she just can't make the first move. There's that fear again.

When I first spoke to Lori about all of this, the idea for this book was still very young and hazy. As the idea became clearer and I began working on the book more and more, I kept thinking of Lori. One night she invited me to dinner at her house. Since I knew how great a cook she was, I jumped at the invitation. During dinner, we were talking about life in general. It seemed that although Lori has a great job that pays a salary that would make you drool, she still was always short of money. Her car and house were really doing a number on her bank account and she hadn't had a vacation in a long time.

Then, one of those little light bulbs went off in my head. Here I was, sitting with a beautiful woman who was a great cook. She needed two things, money and romance. What a natural!

I asked Lori if she had any interest in starting a small business of her own. She said that she never really gave it much thought, but the idea sounded kind of interesting. What did I have in mind?

"How would you like to be surrounded by 15 single men who'll pay you to come to your house to listen to every word you have to say?", I asked Lori. (How's that for an irresistable offer?). She gave me that "give me a break" look.

Well, I was very serious. Not only was Lori a great cook, she also loved to cook. It wasn't a chore for her. She looked forward to cooking, especially for people who enjoyed the results.

Have you caught on to the idea yet? Well, I suggested that Lori run a cooking class right from her home. The lessons would be held once a week for 5 weeks. She would provide the food, utensils and recipes. The men would provide the money. In this case, each man paid $55.00 for the 5 week class.

What a bargain. For $11.00 a week, each of these guys would learn how to cook. They would do the actual cooking at Lori's house and they would be fed!!! What bachelor in his right mind would pass this up.

"How am I going to get single men in the class?", was Lori's very reasonable question. Well, that was the easiest part. All she had to do was run a small ad in the local papers that read "COOKING FOR THE SINGLE MALE - A 5 week course in which you'll learn to cook from a pro and eat the fabulous results. For more information call _____."

In fact, if she had written up a little story about her new business and sent it to the local papers, they would have eaten it up, too. She could have gotten lots of free publicity.

Now what could be much easier. In each class, Lori would gross $825.00, she would be doing what she loves - cooking - and she would be surrounded by 15 single men who are hanging on her every word. Is this just heaven? You bet it is. She didn't even have to leave her house. The men came to her!

If she had any concerns about safety, having strangers in her house, having the men know where she lives, etc., she could just as easily have suggested to her local adult school that she run the course through them. She probably would have made less money, but she would have been more secure. But either way, she would have had her cake and gotten to eat it too! What did she have to lose?

This can be done by a man just as easily. All he would have to do is change the name of the class to "Cooking For the Single Woman"!

Now, let's take a look at what you can offer. What skill do you have that would interest the opposite sex? (Not that. Save that for later!). Come on, think harder. If you say "nothing", you're just not thinking. Everyone can teach something. Cooking, carpentry, French, tennis, home repair, karate (there's a good one), dancing, singing, acting, finances, investing, real estate, public speaking, massage (now there's a great one!!). This list could go on almost forever. Think of all the things you know or the things you do. Offer to show someone else how to do it. There, now you're ready to go. You're a teacher.

If you're afraid that you don't know enough about what you'll be teaching, have no fear. The person you'll be teaching knows even less. After all, an expert is just someone who knows more about something than you do.

A while back, I taught high school psychology, earth science and sex education. I had never taught before. So, before school began, I studied up on each of the subjects. I expanded my range of knowledge. I could have gone on Jeopardy and won the grand prize in any of the three categories. I still wasn't sure I knew enough.

Then, classes started. It was only then that I realized that what I had forgotten about the subjects was more than these kids knew! That's why they were in these classes - they didn't know anything about them.

And so it is with your new French student, or your new tennis student. They are coming to you to learn. They don't know anything about what you know.

OK. That's enough about this idea. Now, go out and try it. It works!

Chapter 5

A FREE DATING SERVICE?

Isn't it amazing how some people want life served to them on a silver platter? Any effort on their part is a major inconvenience. I'm sure people in this category could have just read about Lori's method of being Outrageously Successful With the Opposite Sex and come up with a list of problems with the idea. Well, you would have to go shopping each week. You would have to come up with recipes. You would have to clean the kitchen. What if you weren't interested in any of the guys in class, and on and on.

Well, frankly I'm not so sure these people have much chance for success in the single world anyway. If pure luck is on their side, they'll stumble across someone they're compatible with. If not, they'll continue to complain.

What does all of this have to do with this next method? Well, if you wanted life even easier than Lori has it, this may be the method for you. When I heard about this method, I split my sides laughing. It's funny, but it's also brilliant!

The guy who popped up with this idea was having the typical dating problems. He hated bars. He wasn't meeting the right women. He was frustrated. He figured that if he could increase the number of women he was meeting, he would increase his chances of meeting the woman that would knock his socks off. It took no genius to come up with that thought! The problem was how to increase the number of women he was meeting.

He dabbled with a few ideas which really didn't go anywhere. Then, he came up with the jackpot idea. On a plain piece of 8 1/2 x 11" typing paper he very attractively lettered these words at the top of the page...

"FREE DATING SERVICE!"

The letters were large and bold and took up almost 1/3 of the page. Under this headline, he typed in some further information. He said, "If you'll fill out this form and send along a photo of yourself, we'll do our best to match you with someone you'll enjoy. There's absolutely no cost for this service."

He then typed out several questions. They included name, address, phone number, height, weight, interests and so on. In fact, the rest of the questions were very similar to the questions on most dating service applications. Finally, he listed a post office address to send the questionnaires.

The next stop for this genius was the printer. He had 1,000 copies of this flyer printed up. The cost was about $30.00. Then he took the flyers and tacked them up anywhere he could. He used bulletin boards at colleges, supermarkets, banks, etc. He made them available at singles functions. He really let his imagination go wild. Then he waited. His job was done.

As singles would pass the flyers, the headline would grab them. They would take an application and fill it out, figuring they had nothing to lose. Soon, the completed applications started coming in. Men and women of all ages, builds and backgrounds sent in the forms.

Well, obviously, who was the dating service? Right, HE WAS! He would sort through the forms, pick out the ones that appealed to him and make the calls. What about the rest? Well, he would call his friends, both male and female, tell them about his brilliant idea and invite them over to sort through the others. They could pick the people that interested them, as long as they promised to call them. Not only did his social life skyrocket but he also had a list of friends waiting for the next batch of forms to sort through.

If he wanted to narrow down the responses, his headline could have read "WOMEN - FREE DATING SERVICE". Or even "WOMEN 21-40 - FREE DATING SERVICE". This idea works just as well for men as for women. No, let me change that. Now that I give it more thought, this idea would work well for men and incredibly well for women. Men would respond to this idea in greater numbers than women. But, in any event, both men and women will be thrilled with the results.

This idea made everybody happy...the genius who came up with the idea, the women he contacted, his friends, the people they contacted. No money changed hands.

This idea isn't for you? (You've still got to admit it's brilliant!). How about other approaches that are somewhat similar - like running seminars. They can either be specifically for singles or for the general public. You can charge for them or make them free. Either way, you are getting lots of people coming to you, instead of you having to go after them. You may have the simply wonderful task of picking who you want!

What would your seminar be about? How about singles travel, investment, insurance, fitness, nutrition. Are you a chiropractor or a massage therapist? Yes? You've hit the jackpot. Your seminars are naturals.

Think! Where do you fit in here? We have the whole gamut - from the very private one-to-one dating service idea to the public seminar idea. There has to be a place for you there. You are only limited by your imagination.

Ah, creativity. It's so exciting and it's so well rewarded!   And just what do you have to lose?

PAUSE

Every once in a while we'll pause. I'll have a point to make. An important point. Here's the first one.

Already in the first few chapters I've given you a stack of ideas. What do you think about them? Useful? Funny? Ingenious? Inventive?

Those feelings are all great. You have the right attitude. Maybe none of these first ideas are 3 star ideas for you. If not, let me assure you, they are coming. Keep reading.

If you found a 3 star idea already, you probably aren't reading this. You probably are putting it to work. Or maybe you've attained that success you wanted and you're with that person of your dreams. I give you a standing ovation for that.

On the other hand, if you have the feeling that you're just too sophisticated for these ideas - or if you feel that the ideas are ridiculous, juvenile or useless, I've got a good idea as to why you're having problems. You've got an attitude adjustment to make. In the introduction of this book I warned you that if you have a hardened attitude toward meeting the opposite sex, I won't be able to help you unless you put that attitude aside - even for just a while. You may not have hit upon the great idea you want yet, but you will. Loosen up and admire these people for their genius.

We'll take another pause in a while. Keep reading.

Chapter 6

RESPONDING TO PERSONAL ADS?
HERE'S THE SECRET!

What do you think of when I say the words "personal ads"? Losers, weenies, crazies, perverts? Boy, are you wrong. So was I.

When I first started to work on this book, I knew I had to look into the personal ads. Whenever people think of singles trying to meet, talk about the personal ads can't be far behind. I'd heard all of the negative things about the personal ads, too. But I also knew that they couldn't have lasted as long as they have unless there was something good about them. So, off to work I went.

I was flipping through the pages of a local paper when I saw an ad for a free seminar about personal ads. There would be a panel of speakers, each one talking about some aspect of personals. There would be books and tapes available for sale. Best of all, there would be hundreds of people who've either placed personal ads or who were interested in placing ads. My work would be easy.

The day of the seminar came. I packed up and headed out, full of expectations of what I would find. Like most other people, I expected to see a room full of losers - the walking wounded - people who had little to offer and little direction - people who needed the ads. (Is that about as demeaning as I can get?)

I WALKED INTO THE SEMINAR ROOM AND
MY MOUTH DROPPED OPEN!

The room was filled with hundreds of people who appeared quite normal. I started to talk and to listen. They were normal. Very normal in fact! They were roaming around before the seminar, talking about investments, sports, computers, cooking, vacations, graduate degrees. It certainly wasn't the talk of black leather masks, whips, orgies and other curious behavior I had expected to hear. (For those of you hoping that this is what you'd find in the personals - sorry!) Then the seminar began.

There were talks about the busy lifestyles of people today. The best ways to approach the personals was discussed. People were talking about the problems they had with the personals and how they solved them. They also talked about the terrific people they'd met through the personals. Some even had those people with them as proof! What an undiscovered jackpot this was going to be. I left that seminar as a born-again personals fan!

A few days after the seminar, I had to leave the country. I was heading for Barbados for a few weeks. As I was getting on the plane, I grabbed a copy of a publication that had lots of personals. As we flew to Barbados, I devoured each ad. I wanted to see how people would reach out in their ad to attract the person of their dreams...or even a person they would enjoy spending some time with. Lots of them followed what seemed to be a pre-agreed upon style. "SWM, 35, attractive, sensitive and romantic seeks SWF to match". Not very imaginative, but maybe it did the trick.

As I read column after column of ads, my thoughts were mainly on the information I would grab up here. Then, ZAP, it hit me. The ad that was talking right to me. Not to my brain, but to my heart. It was a simple ad, but its charm dazzled me. The red pen came out and I made a circle around the ad. This ad would be my maiden flight into the personals world.

When I checked into my room at the hotel, I unpacked and then dove back into the paper and right to that ad. I read it again to be sure the thrill was still there. It was! I grabbed a sheet of hotel stationery and started to work on a reply. My brain was spinning with smooth, even brilliant replies, but none of my replies seemed to do the trick. I didn't think this would be so difficult. Finally, I cranked out a reply that I was comfortable with. Then, the problem: the final words in the ad were "Photo a must".

Here I was, thousands of miles from home and not planning to return soon. I searched my wallet and could only find one photo of myself. A few months earlier I had been on a safari into the Amazon jungle. My guide had taken a picture of me sitting in a little dugout canoe with a fishing pole in my hand. I was wearing only a pair of shorts, hadn't had a shower or shave in almost a week and was dripping with perspiration. (Not a great visual, is it?) Well, what the hell! The photo and the letter were put into a hotel envelope. I bought some stamps and off it went.

In the letter to my fantasy woman, I told her I was out of the country. I told her when I'd be back. I apologized for the photo, but mentioned that it was all I had available. I described myself - what I did for a living, my interests, etc. All in all, I thought it was at best only a fairly appealing letter.

I HAD NO IDEA OF HOW APPEALING MY LETTER REALLY WAS!

I was home for less than two hours when the phone rang. It was my personal ad fantasy. Her first words were "You are my hero!".

"Who is this?", was my very reasonable reply.

She told me it was her ad I answered and then gave me the details on why I was her hero.

She had received almost 100 replies and had answered only one - mine. Why? All of the other replies were so routine. They all were in the typical white envelopes. They said the same old thing. The photos that were sent were all "graduation" pictures. You know the kind - jacket and tie, head turned to the right, phony smile. So, in this stack of replies is my letter. A pale blue envelope, strange shape, very strange stamps, with a return address from Barbados. Inside is a photo of a guy who looks something like the "missing link". It turns out to be a photo from the Amazon jungle.

"Your letter was full of excitement! It looked exciting, it sounded exciting...and I knew you couldn't look as bad in person as you did in that photo". We talked for about half an hour and made arrangements to meet. Neither of us were disappointed. My first venture into "the personals" was a thrill. It also gave me one of the most important bits of information I was looking for.

My personals fantasy lady gave me the word I would continue to jump on throughout my work on this book. The word is "exciting". Be exciting! Think exciting! Act exciting!

I wanted to test this approach one more time. The next time I travelled out of the country I had 30 copies of that Amazon photo made. (Don't laugh). I left loaded with publications having personal ads. This time I was going to Antigua. As soon as my underwear was packed away, I started writing letters. All of the photos were used and 30 letters were on their way back to the States. The letters were basically the same. I just added a few comments about the lady's ad to each of the letters. I couldn't wait to get home.

I wasn't disappointed.

Of the 30 ads I answered, 23 women called. Almost every one of them used the word "exciting" when they talked about my reply to them. This was it. I discovered the "secret".

"Now wait a minute", you say. "I haven't been to the Amazon jungle and I don't have plans to leave the country to get foreign hotel stationery. So what can I do?".

Every one of us is exciting in his or her own way. You start by recognizing just that. If you're going to talk about something, talk about the things you love. You'll just naturally talk with more fire and enthusiasm. If you're going to send a photo, don't send the typical "yearbook" style photo. Send a picture of you doing something. Whether it's zooming down a waterslide, jogging, riding a bike, playing tennis or just about anything but just sitting or standing waiting for your photo to be taken. Action shots show that you're an action person. This gives the person looking at your photo the feeling that you at least have SOME zest for life. That zest you are showing may be exactly what other people want to share. I don't care if you like to stay home and knit. If you have a photo showing you at home knitting with a big smile on your face, it will be appealing to the type of person you want to meet. Be proud of what you're happy doing. Now,

ONE MAJOR WARNING!!!

Do not, under any circumstances, send out a photo of you and your former boyfriend or girlfriend with their part of the photo cut away. You don't think it happens, you say? I can show you a stack of them. Don't do it!

Once you've found a photo that you like, have 100 copies made. It's just not that expensive. As this is being written, I'm looking at an ad that offers to reprint 100 copies of a photo for $22.00. Believe me, you're worth it. Having 100 copies of this photo made up also does something else. It commits you just a little more to this whole process. If you don't answer ads and start sending out photos, you'll be stuck with 100 photos of yourself that you spent good money on. If nothing else, that'll irritate you into sending them out so that they're not wasted.

By the way, should you even bother to send a photo? Absolutely! I don't care what all the altruists say. If you're not attracted to a person's looks, it's an uphill struggle from there.

Send the photo!

You'll get fewer replies, but the ones who do reply will have much more of an interest.

Now, put together a letter you'll use to respond to the ads. Don't send the same letter to each ad. Instead, make the letter more of an outline. Then, you can fill in some details that really respond to the specific ad.

How about an example of a response letter?

OK. Here's a letter with some blank spaces. The spaces would be filled in with some details about the particular ad you are responding to.

```
Dear _____,

    Your ad in _____ really caught my eye, so I
had to respond to find out more about you.  My
name is _____, I'm ___ years old, divorced
with __ children.  I'm ___ tall and weigh ___.

    In your ad you mention that you like to
_____.  That's one of my real passions.  In
fact, just two weeks ago I _____.  I had the
time of my life.

    I've enclosed a recent photo of myself.  It
was taken just a few weeks ago as I was
walking off the tennis courts near my home.
Actually I don't perspire that much normally.
It was just a really tough match (I lost, but
it was really a close one).

    If you'd like to talk a while, why not give
me a call at _____ anytime after 6 PM.  Or,
you can send a note and a photo of yourself
to: Box 12345, _____.

Looking forward to hearing from you.
```

This is a fairly simple outline letter that can be changed each time to fit the ad you are responding to. When you write, just give your first name. You may not want to give out your phone number right away. That's fine. You may also want to use a Post Office box for first time replies. That's also just fine. Both practices are very common and quite accepted.

The biggest mistake people make with the personals, though, is not even trying them. They listen to stories from their friends and decide that, based on that second hand information, personals are not for them. Well, that's just nonsense. Give it a good shot. It only costs a few stamps, a few photos and a few hours?

Personals work...if you work them!

Well, what do you have to lose?

OVER 1 MILLION QUALITY SINGLES
across America will read your personal ad when you place a NATIONAL PERSONAL AD with the Singles Press Association* !!!

Through a special National Personal Ad Co-op Program established by the Singles Press Association, your personal ad will appear in 24 QUALITY singles publications from New York to California. It's fun and easy to participate in this fantastic opportunity.

1. Write your personal ad—**50 WORDS OR LESS**—in the space provided below and fill in your name and address (for office use only—ads are all printed with code numbers only).

2. Send it with a check for **$175** payable to Lifestyles Publishing. (If you submitted your ad independently to these publications it would cost you several hundred dollars more.)

3. **MAIL TO: SINGLES PRESS ASSOC. CO-OP c/o LIFESTYLES PUBLISHING 300 MT. LEBANON BLVD. #210-B PITTSBURGH, PA 15234-1507 PHONE (412) 561-2277**

A copy of your personal ad will immediately be sent to the following 24 participating Singles Press Assoc. member publications and your ad will appear in the earliest possible issue of each. You'll also receive free copies of those issues.

- *PITTSBURGH SINGLES' LIFESTYLES*, AND
- *PGH.'S FINEST PERSONALS*, 300 Mt. Lebanon Blvd. #210-B, Pittsburgh PA 15234, $6.95 6 mo trial subscription (you'll get both above publications), $3 sample
- *SINGLES ALMANAC*, 138 Brighton Ave., #209 Boston MA 02134, $12 yr, smpl $1
- *SMOKING SINGLES*, 331 W. 57th St. #165, New York NY 10019, $18 yr, smpl $3 (can be excluded if you wish)
- *DATE BOOK*, PO Box 473, Pleasantville NY 10570, $21 yr, smpl $2
- *METROLINA SINGLES MAGAZINE*, PO Box 11627, Charlotte NC 28220, $16 yr/$3
- *SINGLES' SERENDIPITY*, PO Box 5794, Jacksonville FL 32247, $11 yr, smpl $2.50
- *TODAY'S SINGLE*, PO Box 293098 Nashville TN 37229, $12 yr, smpl $1
- *TENNESSEE SINGLE LIFE*, PO Box 50711, Knoxville TN 37950, $10.99 yr, smpl $3
- *COLUMBUS SINGLE SCENE*, PO Box 30856, Gahanna OH 43230, $20 yr, smpl $2
- *OHIO'S FINEST SINGLES NEWS & VIEWS*, Box 770610, Cleveland OH 44107, $12/$2
- *CAROL'S SINGLES*, PO Box 13500, Akron OH 44334, $14 yr, smpl $2
- *CHRISTIAN SINGLES NEWS*, PO Box 100, Harrison OH 45030, $23 yr, $2
- *SINGLE FILE*, PO Box 6706, Grand Rapids MI 49516, $12 yr, smpl $2
- *SINGLE LIVING*, PO Box 573, Ames IA 50010, $12 yr, $2
- *SOLO RFD*, 318 S. Main, Sioux Falls SD 57102, $15/$1, free past iss. 800-UALONE2
- *SWEETHEART*, PO Box 514, St. Ignatius MT 59865, $15 yr, smpl $2
- *SINGLES CHOICE*, 113 McHenry Rd., Buffalo Grove IL 60089 (Chicago), $12 yr,$3
- *SELETEDSINGLES*, PO Box 40981, Baton Rouge LA 70835, $15 yr, smpl $2
- *GET-TWO-GETHER*, PO Box 1413, Fort Collins CO 80522, $15yr/$3
- *SINGLESLINE*, PO Box 16005, Colorado Springs CO 80935, $12 yr, smpl $2
- *SINGLE SCENE (AZ Solo)*, 7432 E. Diamond, Scottsdale AZ 85257, $8.50/$1
- *ARIZONA SINGLES*, PO Box 3424, Flagstaff AZ 86003, $15 yr, $2
- *SINGLE MAGAZINE & ENTERTAINMENT GUIDE*, PO Box 5709, San Diego CA 92165, $6 yr, smpl $2

* All Singles Press Association publications adhere to the high standards, ethics and service codes established and monitored by that organization.

SINGLES PRESS ASSOCIATION NATIONAL PERSONAL AD (50 words or less)

_____
_____
_____
_____
_____
_____
_____
_____
_____
_____
_____
_____
_____
_____
_____
_____

The following information is kept strictly confidential!

FULL NAME _____

ADDRESS & APT # _____

CITY, STATE & ZIP _____

HOME PHONE (_____) _____

Send this with $175 to: 300 Mt. Lebanon Blvd #210-B, Pittsburgh PA 15234

Some publications that include 900 phone options may contact you further about option choices.

Chapter 7

HOW TO WRITE PERSONAL ADS THAT WILL
JAM YOUR MAILBOX WITH REPLIES

I want to stay with the personals for just a while longer. In this chapter let's talk about running ads - that really will boost your chances of outrageous success.

First, let's talk about all the excuses people have for not running their own ads. "They" say that all you hear from are nuts and perverts. Nothing could be further from the truth. Yes, you will get your share of strange replies, but the number will be small.

"They" say that you'll get strange phone calls and stranger people knocking on your door at all hours of the night. Nonsense! You'll only give out your phone number and address to people you've met in a neutral place. You'll make arrangements to meet somewhere for a short time to get to know each other. If that works out well and you're confident that you're dealing with someone you'd like to spend more time with, you take it from there. How is this different from what you do when you meet an appealing man or woman some other way?

Right. It isn't different.

"They" say that your friends will recognize your ad and ridicule you. Mule muffins! Look through the last ten issues of your local personal ads and see if you have the slightest idea who ANY ONE person is. Of course you can't. And even if, by some miracle, your friends did know it was you - what's the problem?

COKE AND PEPSI CAN ADVERTISE
WHY CAN'T YOU?

You're taking definite action for your own happiness. Watch who'll be smiling when you are spending lots of time snuggling up with that terrific person you found through the personals!

So, how do you get started? Begin with the first line of the ad and simply go from there. Make the first line interesting. Maybe a little intriguing. Here's one you can use - "Cinderella is seeking a charming prince to take her to the ball". Or, if you're a male - "Prince Charming...".

By all means, avoid the standard "SWF, 34, attractive, sensitive, seeks same style SWM". Boy that really sparks my interest! I can't wait to meet the exciting person who dreamed up that witty ad!

After your first line, which can be cute, sincere, outrageous but by all means interesting, give some details about yourself. FOR GOD'S SAKE BE HONEST! Don't say that you're in great shape if you have some serious weight to lose. Don't say you love kids if you don't. Don't say you are a headturning knockout that leaves men panting unless you can back it up. Just be honest. Just be pleased that you are you. Remember, you're going to want to meet the people that answer your ad. It's much better to understate things just a bit and have people pleasantly surprised when they meet you than to give a big build up to something you can't back up.

Give the people reading your ad a little idea of what you generally like to do. Don't say things like: "I like peanut butter, puppies, the Big Dipper, rainbows and new shoes." I'm not sure if I'm dealing with a space cadet left over from the 1960's or someone who can't think of anything they are really interested in. Be specific, but be clear.

For example: "Camping is one of my real passions" or "The opera and classical music are two undying loves in my life. Will you be the third?". Put some power into your words. Let people know that you're energetic and exciting. I've read thousands and thousands of personal ads and, frankly, most of them are deadly boring.

Again, I want to be clear: you do not have to be out climbing mountains, sky diving and parasailing every day to be outrageously successful with the opposite sex. Just have some good feelings for what you are doing and what you like to do, even if it's watching TV seven nights a week.

After you've written the ad, you may want to close with some of the things you want. You might say "Phone number and photo please", "Photo helpful", "Photo appreciated", "No photo, no reply" or whatever else you want. I've found that photos are important to me. You decide what's important to you and ask for it!

Just as an aside, I've been told that one of the most successful personal ads ever run in one major publication simply had two words. The words were "Mr. Wrong" followed by a box number. He got an avalanche of replies. After the man who ran this ad ran out of women, he ran a second ad, which pulled even better. It had four words - "Mr. Wrong is back". I'm not really sure what this has to say for the women who responded to the ads. I'm just reporting the results. The point is that when the ad is unusual, interesting, exciting, etc. the response will probably be a whole lot better than a routine "SWM, 38" type ad. Be different, be daring. What's there to lose? If the ad bombs, you just run another one.

What happens when you start getting replies? Sort through them and pick out the ones you feel good about. Here's some important advice:

GO WITH YOUR INSTINCTS!

So many times we have a hunch about something or someone that we ignore. Trust your feelings and instincts. Once you learn to tune into these feelings, you'll be surprised how often they're right.

So, if you're going through your replies and your instincts tell you to pass on one particular person, do it. There will be more. The same holds true for when you call someone. If your instincts tell you that this is going nowhere, politely end it. Don't feel obligated to meet the person just because they answered your ad. Your first call is really just a fact-finding mission. You want to talk to the person to see if there's a genuine "flow". If there is, if you find it's easy and enjoyable to talk with the person, set up a meeting. Arrange to meet somewhere neutral, such as in a park (ooo, they can be romantic!), for a short amount of time. If you really hit it off well, you can stay longer. But, if things just don't work out, you don't have to stay for an awkwardly long amount of time.

If things work out well the first time you meet, take it from there the way you would any other second date.

Being a good journalist, I had to run my own ads and report on the results.

As I said, avoid the same, boring beginnings. I did.

I have a real love for redheads. No, a real passion for redheads. I don't know why. And that doesn't mean that I don't like blondes, brunettes, etc. I love them, too. But, red hair is a little bonus.

As you know, redheads are fairly scarce. So, I thought this would be perfect. I'll advertise for a redhead. I started the ad with the truth. The first words were: "REDHEADS REALLY TURN ME ON!". I followed with "Slim, fit, non-smoking redhead with top notch looks, brains & personality sought by a very handsome, exciting, devilish SWM who promises romance, adventure & magic."

That was it. Then I waited.

I got just what I wanted. Redheads. Attractive, intelligent, exciting redheads. Lots of them!!!

Let your ads work for you. Don't try to be everything to everybody. Be specific. Do you like redheads too? Say so. You just may be swimming in redheads.

How about smokers. Do you care? Say so.

How about height, weight, religion, interests and so on. Make yourself happy. You're paying for the ad.

If you just want some company, a very general ad will get lots of replies. If you want to be thrilled, advertise for exactly what turns you on. As always, you won't get as many replies. But the ones you do get will be close to exactly what you want. You should be in heaven! What an easy, cheap way to find the man or woman (or men or women) of your dreams!!!

One thing we haven't mentioned is what to do with the replies that don't interest you.

You'll have, in your hands, letters from people who are looking for other people. Don't let them go.

You have friends. Your friends may be looking. Have you ever wanted to be a matchmaker? Here's your chance. Give your friends the letters of the people who don't interest you. Let them follow up.

If you are tall, blond and thin and your friends are just the opposite, be sure to have them tell the letter writer who they are and why they're calling so that they won't be surprised. The letter writer expects you. They know something about you from your ad. This doesn't mean that they won't be interested in your friends. You never know until you ask.

This even works when you answer one of the letters with a phone call.

You get a response to your ad. The letter sounds interesting. You call the person. For whatever reason, after speaking with them, you feel that this person is not for you. SAY SO! Don't keep wandering forever without getting to the point. Tell the person that you don't think things will work between you two...

BUT!

Quickly add that you have a friend who might be just what they're looking for. Offer to pass on this person's phone number to a friend and see what happens.

When I called one of my redheads, this is exactly what happened. The woman was truly delightful on the phone...intelligent, interesting. But for other reasons, I was sure that this would go no where. I told her. I also offered to pass her letter and number to my good friend, who I could highly recommend.

She was impressed...and interested. In fact, she quickly followed by describing a friend of hers that I might be interested in. I was. We made the switch!

Never give up on a situation! Always think about how it can be turned into a winner...there's got to be a way.

As I've said a number of times so far and I'll say a number of times again, one of the biggest reasons people don't have great success in meeting is simply that they're afraid. They're afraid to try different things - afraid of failing, afraid of being hurt or embarrassed. But remember, "When you ain't got nothin', you got nothin' to lose".

Good Places to Put Your Personal Ads

Here's a list of several singles publications around the country. You'll find the name of the publication, the address, the cost of a sample copy and the subscription rate. I've spoken with the people who put out each and every one of these publications. They're all delightful. Send for sample copies, then subscribe to the ones you enjoy. You'll find more information about each of these publications throughout the book. I can recommend them all without reservation.

Active Singles Life
3450 6th Avenue, South
Seattle, WA 98134
Sample copy: $1.50
Subscription: $14/year

Singles Almanac
725 Route 440
Jersey City, NJ 07304
Sample copy: $2.00
Subscription: $22/year

The Florida Singles Entertainer
Box 76085
Ocala, FL 32676
Sample copy: $1.00
Subscription: $18/year

Smoking Singles
331 W. 57th St., Suite 165
New York, NY 10019
Sample copy: $3.00
Subscription: $18/year

Metro Singles
Box 28203
Kansas City, MO 64118
Sample copy: $3.00
Subscription: $12/4 issues

The Tucson Connection
Box 15114
Tucson, AZ 85708
Sample copy: $1.00
Subscription: $8/year

Carol's Singles
Box 13500
Akron, OH 44334
Sample copy: $2.00
Subscription: $14/year

Jewish Singles Magazine
7320 SW 82nd St., #B201
Miami, FL 33143
Sample: 900-446-2228 ($.95/min)
Subscription: $20/year

Pittsburgh Singles' Lifestyles
300 Mt. Lebanon Blvd., #210-B
Pittsburgh, PA 15234
Sample copy: $3.00
Subscription: $6.95/6 months

Singles Link
8034 South Yale, Suite 172
Tulsa, OK 74136
Sample copy: $2.00
Subscription: $10/year

Tennessee Single Life Magazine
Box 50711
Knoxville, TN 37950
Sample copy: $3.00
Subscription: $10.99/year

U.S. Singles Today
300 First Interstate Bank Bldg.
Box 927
Bedford, TX 76095
Sample copy: $1.00

Chapter 8

LOVE AND LEARN

I like to dance. I don't particularly like going to a disco and dancing. I prefer jazz, modern, tap and so forth. So, I took a jazz dancing course at a local adult school. I went to learn jazz dancing. I learned a whole lot more than just dancing.

While I was looking through my local adult school catalog I noticed a course called "Basic Jazz Dancing". Sounded interesting. I called for some more information about the course. The woman on the other end of the phone gave me the information I wanted, but had a bit of a strange tone to her voice.

Oh, well.

I registered for the course.

When I mentioned the course to a friend I got a strange look. "Do you know that course is for women?", she asked. Actually, I thought it was for people who wanted to learn jazz dancing. "Well, it is, but I've never seen a man in that course.". My eyes lit up! I originally was interested in starting the course. Now, I couldn't wait. Could this be true? Could I be in for 10 weeks of treading water in a sea of dancing delights? (Oh, OK. So that was terrible.)

It was true. The first night of the course was here. I walked into the room and found 14 women...and me. Have I been living in a fog for all these years? How could I not have known about this paradise for single men. What was I going to do with this information? I knew what I was going to do with the class and the benefits. But what about this information.

Well, I'm a kind, generous guy. I'm the type of person who doesn't mind sharing information.

BUT I'M NOT NUTS!

I kept this a secret.

I spent 10 weeks learning jazz dancing, with an ear to ear smile every minute of every class. Needless to say, I had no trouble getting a date for a good while.

You've probably already heard this a thousand times. Women - take a class designed for men. Men - take a class designed for women. Still, we don't do it. I didn't do it. I fell into this strategy by accident. Why? I don't know. Maybe we are embarrassed going into a room where you are the only representative of your gender. Maybe we really don't want to hit the jackpot. You know, that whole "fear of success" thing. Who knows?

Now I don't have to tell you that I did a whole lot more research in this area. I took a cooking class. In fact, I took two. Other classes followed that first jazz class. All of the classes, though, were on subjects I really wanted to learn. I didn't sit through a sewing class just to be surrounded by women. I just don't want to learn too much about sewing. I did want to learn more about cooking, though. I wanted to learn more about dancing. Being surrounded by women was that added benefit.

Men, the classes you may be interested in are obvious. Women, the classes are just as obvious - construction and home repair classes, automotive classes, etc. Volleyball classes are great! You might also want to consider financial, real estate and small business classes as well. While they're not exclusively male classes, there is a high percentage of males. Often, the men in these classes are fairly interesting, motivated doers. The people who take these classes often are people who want to move in the world. Why not hook up with the motion and share what you have to offer?

What can you expect when you take "an opposite sex" class? Well, from my experience, when a woman takes a male-oriented class, she is quickly surrounded by men who "want to help". They want to show you how to hold the wrench or some short cuts to building that shelf. The competition among the men will be open and obvious.

When a man takes a female oriented class, something different happens. When you first walk in, you get quick, sly glances. Women rarely approach men with the same vigor that men approach women. They are more subtle. As the class goes on, they will casually dance in front of you. They will casually suggest that you use different cooking utensils for the dish you are preparing. But, rest assured that they have just as much interest! They simply exhibit it in a different way. The competition among the women will not be as obvious, but it will be there just as intensely.

Putting yourself in the right situation seems to be one of the simplest methods for standing out. Not only as a male or a female, but simply as a person.

There's an old story about a man who owned a large construction company. He had hundreds of people working for him. At each construction site, he would set up an office with a large window so that he could watch the construction going on.

Eventually it came time to promote one of the workers to a supervisory position. He called in his managers. They all looked out the window as the boss pointed to the man he was going to promote. It was easy to pick him out. He was wearing a bright red shirt. Everyone else was wearing the typical green and tan shirts. It was also very obvious that he was working at full capacity. He got the promotion.

A while later, his friends asked him why it was he that got the promotion.

His reply was very simple.

He said: "I wear a red shirt and I work like hell."

THIS MAN HAD <u>THE PERFECT STRATEGY!</u>

He wore a red shirt. This bright color stood out in the sea of duller green and tan shirts. Now that he had people's attention, he took advantage of the situation by working like hell.

That's a winning combination that'll work for you!

But, you have to stand out in some other way. This book is full of "red shirts" you can wear.

It's up to you to work like hell.

What are you waiting for? You have nothing to lose!

Chapter 9

HOW TO SURROUND YOURSELF WITH THE OPPOSITE SEX AND GET PAID TO DO IT!

Have you ever taken tennis lessons or piano lessons or, for that matter, any type of lesson? Expensive, isn't it?

What are you good at? What kind of lessons could you offer? Oh, come on. We're all good at something. We can all teach something. You don't have to be a world class bowler to teach bowling. You just have to be better than the person you are teaching.

Could you teach some sport? Could you teach cooking, or a foreign language, or speed reading? How about investing, meditation, nutrition? The list could go on and on. Use that hidden talent you have.

There are two ways to approach this. You can think about what you can teach and then offer it to people. Or, if you are a bit more outrageous, you can think about the type of person you want to meet and think about what you can offer them. Do you want to meet college students? Do you want to meet teachers, doctors, stockbrokers or retired people? Let's look into some approaches.

Let's say you feel comfortable teaching French. Now, you wouldn't qualify for a job as a translator at the UN, but you could certainly get by well enough if you were dropped off in Paris. You feel a little nervous about teaching someone, but that's just natural. You'll survive this.

You know that if someone wants to take French lessons, they'll have to take a serious look at their bank account. The lessons are not going to come cheap...until now, that is.

Before you offer your lessons, check out the going prices of French lessons in your area. Suppose you find the going rate is $30.00 per hour. Now, you're set. Your French lessons are going to be an incredible bargain at just $10.00 an hour. That should get the phone ringing. Anyone who wants to learn French has probably already done some price shopping. Your ad clearly says that you charge only $10.00. People should start calling.

The phone rings. It's a man interested in taking French lessons. You are a woman. You now have your first student. You have a man willing to pay you $10.00 to be with you for an hour. Not bad!

The phone rings again. It's a woman interested in taking French lessons. You are a woman. Unfortunately, you just don't have any openings in your schedule for another student.

The phone rings a third time. It's a man interested in taking French lessons. You are a woman. You just found an opening in your schedule for another student. You have another man interested in paying you $10.00 an hour to be with you.

Can you rearrange this idea to suit your needs? What if you'd like to meet a business executive? Simple. Just think about what would be useful for this group to learn. Maybe it would be time management; maybe organizational skills; maybe gift buying...or wardrobe coordination. The list is long. Once you think of what they could use, go down your list and think about what you could offer. You now have an instant "in" to that group of people. You're using one of the basic principles of being outrageously successful with the opposite sex. You are surrounding yourself with the type of people you want to meet...and getting paid to do it!

Men and women can use this idea with equal success. It's an "equal opportunity" idea!

You can do this with any group of people: nurses, teachers, tall people, short people, athletes, musicians. They all have something they'd like to improve. If you can teach it, and make the lessons cheaper than normal, you're putting yourself in an enviable position. Get to work! You have nothing to lose.

Chapter 10

DON'T BE A VICTIM

Another no-fail rule for being outrageously successful with the opposite sex is: "Don't be a victim of the system, BE the system!".

Let me explain.

Lots of singles pore through the newspaper listings of singles events - the parties, socials, dances, "rap groups", (that's a dated term!), etc. They look for something that sounds at least a little interesting. Once they've decided what to attend, they suit up and head out. They walk in the door and often find dozens of other people. At some of these events, they'are part of a group of hundreds of other people. They disappear into the crowd.

This is a perfect example of being "part of the system". The people attending these events are just one tiny part of a large crowd. The entire crowd is competing with each other for the same thing. While this may work well for some people, it's just not my idea of fun...and I'll bet it's not one of yours, either.

The people putting these groups together are just like you and I. They generally have no special skills, background, talents, etc. They simply wanted to approach the singles field with an upper hand. They wanted to meet a particular type of person, so they started a group of singles with that special interest. They knew that they would not succeed as well if they were just part of the system. They had to BE the system.

So, they organized a group of hikers, small business owners, sports oriented people or whatever. It didn't take much. They found a place to meet and put together some flyers announcing the group. If people didn't come, they tried a different approach. (Did you catch what I just said? Let me repeat it. "They tried a different approach." This is a continuing theme of this book. It should also be a continuing theme in your life. If one thing doesn't work, try another.)

What'is so important about this idea? As I mentioned, if you just go to a singles event, you're really at the mercy of the people who organized the function. You're also at the mercy of the people at the function. If you want to be in a group of single small business owners, unless you can find that specific group, you'll have to weed them out of the functions you do attend. You become just a very small fraction of a larger group.

But, if you put the group together, you benefit in a lot of ways. You pick the type of group that will attend. If you only want people over 50, that's how you announce the group. Do you only want people over a certain height, or of a particular religion, or even of a particular nationality? You can do it.

The other BIG benefit is that when you organize the group, you will be the center of attention. When questions come up, you are the person people look for. When new people come, you are the first to meet and welcome them. You're the leader. You're in charge. You now have one thing that many people find very attractive - power. You are in control and you're surrounded by exactly the type of person you want. Not a bad place to be, eh?

If your mind boggles at the thought of putting together a group, you're giving in to "I can't" thinking again. Of course you can. Remember,

NO GUTS, NO GLORY!

Just publicize the group, have some very light refreshments, perhaps a speaker or two and the group is under way. The people who get together in your group want an excuse for getting together with other people who are just like them. They'll be happy to help keep the group going. It certainly is in their best interest. Where else will they be able to find a group of single skunk owners under 45 or single people over 6'6" or single people interested in magic.

If your group falls apart, they'll have to search again. Give your imagination a chance to stretch and give yourself credit for the abilities you have. When your group is up, running and successful, have me come and speak to them. You can turn the talk into a great fundraiser. Call me and I'll give you the details.

To close this chapter, I want to again stress that attending singles functions may be fine for lots of people. It may be just what they want and need. They may be very successful at these groups. If that's so, that's fine for them. But, there are lots of singles who don't like these functions. They want something else. They want more control of their lives. For these people, starting a group could be the perfect answer. Getting the group off the ground may not be a bed of roses, but it could pay off VERY well. What do you have to lose?

WHY YOU SHOULD STOP READING
THIS BOOK RIGHT NOW!

So, here we are. You've finished the first 10 chapters of a book called *How to Be Outrageously Successful With the Opposite Sex*.

We talked about the reasons people aren't outrageously successful with the opposite sex...and how they <u>can</u> be -- fairly easily.

We went through the motivational part of the book...the part that told you -- and proved to you -- that you could do it. I showed you the rewards.

You read about people who <u>are</u> outrageously successful with the opposite sex...and the ingenious methods they're using. They were methods that anyone could successfully use. They were all fairly easy. Some took a little courage, but others took no courage at all.

So, if you're sitting here right now, telling yourself how these ideas can't work...they're silly...they're not for you...maybe they're not for anybody. You could never do this. It's just not this easy...

If you are telling yourself that nonsense...

PUT THIS BOOK DOWN RIGHT NOW!

No, even better, put this book back on the shelf. You're wasting your time. You're going to get nowhere.

Put the book away and pick it up again when you're really ready to make the change. I can tell you for sure, <u>it's not now.</u>

Do you want to be sure? Go back and read the first part of this book another time. When you get to this part again, ask yourself how you feel. If you feel the same way, put the book away. You're hopeless...at least for now.

But remember, while your copy of this book is on the shelf, there are thousands of people using these techniques to find lots of great people.

So don't take too long to change your attitude.

STOP THE HIGH COST OF DATING!

Guys, do you ever find yourself spending too much money on dates?
Do you not ask women out sometimes because you're "short of cash?"
Do you think it takes a lot of money to show a woman a good time?

Well, not anymore!

All you need is **The Cheap Date Handbook** — The Complete How-To Guide to Successful Inexpensive Dating.

Learn How To:
- Meet and talk to beautiful women who like **you**, not your wallet
- Be romantic on a budget
- Creatively date without bucks & how a $20 date can be more fun than a $100 one
- Entertain at home & make your apartment a fun, comfortable place women will love... on a budget
- Dress well for a pittance
- Travel anywhere in the world cheaply, using little known tricks like being an Air Courier
- Say what it takes to make a woman like you & want to be with you
- Spot women who like you for you... EVEN FASTER

☞ Tons of tips for single guys, couples, even women on how to stretch your dating $$$
☞ You'll save more than the price of the book with just your first few dates
☞ And much,much more!
☞ Over 170 pages jam packed with ideas
☞ A full sized 8½″ by 11″ inexpensive dating "Bible"

FREE BONUS IF YOU ACT NOW

Order today and receive a special tape cassette worth $14.95 **FREE**, giving extra special money saving dating ideas and tips not covered in the book. You'll be amazed at the knowledge you'll soon possess. Date all the ladies you want... on a budget... and using these creative techniques, they'll love it!

So get the book and the cassette tape for only **$19.95** plus $3.00 shipping and handling. (CA residence add $1.65, or $24.60 total.)

That's probably less than you OVERSPENT on your last date!

STOP THE HIGH COST OF DATING & ORDER TODAY
Send your check or money order to: Ultimate Secrets

Box 43033, Upper Montclair, NJ, 07043

or save time with your **MasterCard** or **Visa** and call: **1-800-688-6283**

Chapter 11

ON A SCALE FROM 1 TO 10...

How about a really outrageous technique? One that may make people wonder if you're playing with a full deck, but one that's really <u>powerful</u>!

A while back, I was reading about sales skills. I was going over what are called "closing techniques". These are strategies salespeople use to get people to sign on the dotted line. The technique I was reading about sounded great. It goes like this.

You're trying to close a sale. You keep saying the right things, but the customer is just meandering. You realize that you <u>must</u> take some drastic action to get things back on the track. So, right in the middle of the conversation you say: "Could I just stop here for a minute and ask you a question? On a scale of one to 10, where 1 means you wish you never came into this place...and 10 means you can't wait to get a pen in your hand to sign this order, where do we stand?". The customer will be a bit startled, since this certainly is an unusual question. In fact, they may think you're kidding, so you'll probably have to repeat it.

"No, Mr. Kennedy, I'm serious. On a scale of 1 to 10 with one meaning you can't stand to hear me utter another word about this product and 10 meaning you can't wait another second to own it, where do we stand?". When the customer realizes that you are serious, he says: "Well, I guess we're at about a 6.".

HERE'S WHERE THE MOST IMPORTANT PART OF THIS TECHNIQUE COMES INTO PLAY.

You say "What do I have to do to get to a 10?". The customer then says: "Well, you'd have to lower your price" or "You'd have to deliver by Monday and give me a free service agreement". Now you know what you have to do to wrap up the sale!!! All you have to do is decide if you want to do it.

Some time after I read about this idea, I was speaking with a woman. Our conversation started out just fine, but quickly began to wander.

A light bulb went on in my mind as I remembered the sales technique.

I figured I had nothing to lose, since this conversation was going nowhere. So, I said: "Can I stop for just a minute and ask you a question? On a scale of 1 to 10, where 1 means you can't bear the sight of me for another second. You want me to walk out that door and disappear from your life forever. And 10 means that you wish I'd stop talking so that we could leave this place and have a night of nuclear energy passion, where do we stand?".

She gave me one of those "get the net" looks. I told her I was serious, so she said: "Well, about an 8".

An 8!!?? I thought we were at about a 2! So, then came the closer. "What do I have to do to get to a 10?".

With an astonished look and a smile that said "If you're crazy enough to ask me this, I'm crazy enough to tell you".

She told me.

The rest is nuclear energy history!

By the way, I heard a joke about this technique. A man is at a bar and sees a gorgeous woman. He starts talking with her. He wants things to move along faster than they are. So he says: "On a scale of 1-10, where 1 means that you can't stand the sight of me & 10 means you can't wait to jump into bed with me, where do I stand?

The woman said: "About an 8."

The man, faithfully following this technique, said: "What do I have to do to get to a 10?".

The woman said: "Give me $50."

Alright, so maybe it doesn't work <u>every</u> time.

Understand that you can adapt this technique in many ways. It can be used by both men and women. You can make 1 and 10 be anything, in any situation. The point is that you're not coming on with <u>the same old routines</u>. That's where most people get lost. They try to figure out the best pick-up lines or the best way to respond to a man. By doing that, they really just fall into that "same old style" trap. Have some fun while you meet these people. Be a bit outrageous. People will love it.

What do you have to lose?

Chapter 12

HOW TO STAND OUT FROM THE CROWD

Sometimes you just fall into good luck. You're not even trying. Good luck is following you around. In fact, you couldn't dodge it if you tried.

That's just what happened to me a while back. In fact, it gave me enough material for this chapter!

I was at a resort in the Carribean that's popular with singles. When I first arrived, I saw the usual. People dressed to kill and strutting like peacocks. Sexy bathing suits and lots of sun tan lotion. A lot of non-verbal positioning.

Now that we're all headed toward being outrageously successful with the opposite sex, we know what was going on there. Everyone was trying to look as perfect and as sexy as could be. Men were competing for the attention of women. Women were competing for the attention of men. Each person thought that he or she was an individual standing out from the crowd. Actually, it was one big arena, with everyone competing at once. No one was really standing out at all, because

NO ONE REALLY PUT THEMSELVES IN A POSITION TO STAND OUT.

That was no place for me, so I left.

I wandered around the resort and found two people up on a trapeze! I walked over and sat down to watch. In just a few moments, one of the men asked me if I wanted to try the trapeze.

I looked around to see who he was talking to.

He was talking to me! Would I like to try the trapeze? You bet your buns I would. The closest I'd ever come to a trapeze was sitting in the 5th row at the circus. I couldn't get up that ladder fast enough!

The first lesson was easy. Just hold onto the bar with both hands and jump off the platform. Nothing to it. We used to do this when we were kids on the monkey bars. I went back and forth a time or two and then bounced down into the net.

Lesson number two. Swing on the bar once. On the second swing, put your legs up on the bar, let go with your hands and swing upside down. A snap. That monkey bar training was REALLY paying off now.

As easy as could be I hooked my legs over the bar. When I was ready, I let my hands go with a little circus flair. As I was swinging upside down, I noticed a bit of a crowd forming. This was the making of a dream come true. Doing circus tricks in front of a crowd.

Lesson number three. As soon as I jump off the platform, holding the bar with my hands, I'm to hook my legs over the bar and hang upside down so that when I swing back toward the platform, I'm already upside down. This had to be done quickly, because on the second swing back, someone on the opposite trapeze would also be hanging upside down and would be coming at me. When we met in the middle, I'd grab his arms with my hands. I'd let go of my legs around my bar and we would both be swinging on his trapeze, him upside down, me right side up, hanging from his arms.

I got ready, held the bar and then jumped. I scrambled to get my legs over the bar and my hands free so that I could hang upside down and watch the platform come back at me. It felt like I had about two seconds to do it, but I did it!

As I was watching the platform come toward me, I noticed the crowd was growing much larger. As I swung back, I saw the upside down hands I was to grab. We met in the middle with a firm lock on each other. I let go of my legs and was swinging in the air, held up only by this character I had never met, hanging upside down on his trapeze. An impressive sight and round of applause came from the crowd. This was my first circus "trick". What a rush. My trapeze partner let me go on signal and I bounced into the net.

Could there be more of a thrill?

Of course! It was lesson four. My grand finale.

I was to jump off my platform, hang upside down, grab onto my other partner, swing once with him back and forth. As we swung back, together, my original trapeze bar would be heading toward us again. When my partner gave the signal, I was to let go of his arms, flip up and spin around and grab MY trapeze bar back to my platform. The crowd loved just HEARING that. They couldn't wait to see it.

Neither could I!

Have you ever performed before a standing room only crowd? Well, neither had I until then. I climbed up the ladder and felt a real rush of excitement. No fear, just thrill. I put chalk on my hands so I wouldn't slip and then grabbed my bar. My partner started his swing. I waited for the signal and then started my swing. Quickly I hung upside down and was ready for the switch. I saw my partner hanging upside down with his arms stretched out, waiting for me. We met in the middle and made a perfect switch. "Remember", he said as we started our swing together, "when I say 'now', let go of my arms, flip up and spin around and just reach out. Your bar will be there.". Somehow that didn't even sound logical, but it was too late. As the Little Rascals said "Hey Stymie, where are you going?". "I don't know, but I'm on my way!".

We were on the way back. My partner said "Ready.......NOW!" I let go, spun around, reached out and for just that one second I was suspended in mid-air, motionless. I looked straight ahead of me and what do you know! There was my bar; right in front of me. I reached out, grabbed it and headed back home. The crowd let out one of those roars you have dreams about. On signal, I let go, bounced into the net and gave one final circus flip off the net and onto the ground.

So, what was the purpose of telling you that whole story? How about the excitement. Did you feel it? You can bet a buck that I did...and so did the crowd.

Very quickly, I found out that my antics on the trapeze were not only thrilling, apparently they were also quite sexy! I immediately became the local celebrity. "Was it hard to do?", "Were you scared?", "Did you ever do that before?".

The point is, everyone else was "doing battle" on the beach with their bathing suits, sunglasses and suntan lotion. I was up on a trapeze, hanging upside down! In fact, more than that. I was the ONLY person on a trapeze, hanging upside down.

IT'S NOT HARD TO STAND OUT WHEN YOU'RE THE ONLY ONE DOING SOMETHIING WITH EVERYONE ELSE WATCHING.

Was this a ploy? Did I really have this all planned out? Well, honestly, no I didn't. I wanted to go on the trapeze. I didn't expect a crowd. I really had no other thoughts. But, my Momma raised no fools. I caught on very quickly to what else was happening. You can make that happen too.

You don't have to swing on a trapeze. Just don't go head-on into the arena and do battle with dozens or hundreds of other people.

Think about how you might stand out and go for it. Do what you do well and don't be afraid to let people see it. Play the piano, juggle, just sit and draw pictures of people passing by, waterski, dance. Folks, I'm talking about <u>anything</u> you do well. When people do something well, it's <u>sexy</u>. Trust me!

As you may be sensing, standing out from the crowd is a major theme of this book. The overwhelming majority of people are doing the same old thing. They're competing against each other. If you stand alone, there's no one to compete against! Stand alone and don't be afraid. You'll only be alone for a short time.

<u>Remember the guy in the red shirt.</u>

What do you have to lose?

Chapter 13

HOW THE PERSONALS CAN FIND YOU LOVE... <u>AND</u> MAKE YOU MONEY

Let's travel back to the personal ads for a while. As you can see, I really think the personals are underrated and under-used. I also feel that the vast majority of people using the ads are doing it the same old way. Once again they make themselves a very small part of a big crowd.

Well, how about another use that can not only bring you some interesting people, but also can make you some money?

One of the biggest barriers that keeps people from using the personals is their fear of actually writing the ad. Most people think they can't write anything well - let alone an ad. Others think that they may be able to write one, but they want something really special or really outrageous. They don't feel they have that talent. Other people want to use the personals, but they simply don't want to write the ads. They know how to write them. They just don't want to. All of these people are giving you a golden opportunity.

How well do you write? Do you think you can write a personal ad? Have you read the ads, and said: "I can do better than that! (After reading this far you <u>should</u> know how to do better!). Here's your chance. Try your hand at writing a few ads. Just make up a person, male or female. Make up a list of interests, height, weight, etc...all of the details. Then, using this imaginary person, write an ad. How does it sound? Not so good? Don't worry about perfection. Try another. Then another and keep on going until you have a flow. Now, visualize a person of the opposite sex. Write an ad for that person. It's becoming easier, isn't it? "Once you have that flow, you're ready to go."

When you have your writing style and ability down, get into business. Run a small ad in the personals column offering to write ads. You could run this business in lots of different ways. You could simply ask the people questions about themselves over the phone. You could put together a little questionnaire asking the information you would want to know to write an effective ad. You could have them send you a picture to get a better idea of what these people look like. Once you've gotten the information together, write an ad or two.

How much do you charge? How much is it worth to you? $15 per ad? $30. Whatever it is, make sure it covers your time and advertising costs and leaves you some money left over.

Now, this is <u>not</u> a manual on how to start a business or how to make money. But, I do have a trick up my sleeve.

HERE'S THE REAL BONUS OF THIS BUSINESS

The money you could make may be nice, but the people you meet may be even nicer! And <u>you'll</u> have first crack at them!

If you're a female and a female wants an ad written, you write the ad, pocket the money and you're on your way. But, when a male wants an ad written, ask for lots of information. Age, height, weight, interests...anything <u>you</u> want to know. If he sounds interesting, get him to send you a picture along with a check for writing the ad.

Since most of your business will be over the phone, a photo will not only help you write the ad, it will also help <u>you</u> decide how much interest you have in him. Of course, the same goes for men writing ads for women. You'll be the first in line for this available male or female. In fact, if things go well, the ad may never get written!

Like most of the other ideas we've gone over so far, this idea blends two strategies - making money and meeting the type of people you want to be with. Also, it's doing something more than just going to the bars on Friday nights, hoping for the best. It's doing something unusual, something more fun than feeling the blues about having no one. It's taking control of your own life.

If it sounds like this idea is going to work for you, hop on it.

You know what I'm going to say next. Right! What do you have to lose?

Chapter 14

LADIES, JUST ASK AND IT'S YOURS!

Women, this chapter is all yours. Men, you can read it and just shake your heads in agreement. But, this chapter is specifically for the women.

Ladies, you have at your disposal a technique for meeting men that's just staggering in its effectiveness. This technique has such a high percentage of success it makes us men "green" with envy. This technique is simple, uses no tricks, no lines and no gimmicks. It can be used at any time and on any one. There is nothing to remember, nothing to forget. This comes as close to a 100% guarantee as you'll find. Best of all, you have something very powerful on your side...the male ego.

Do I have your interest now???

What's this miracle method?

Well, it's simplicity itself. In fact, I don't think it could be simpler.

The secret to getting a man to out with you is -

ASK!!!

Ladies, all you have to do to get us to go out with you is...ask us.

That's right, ask us! Now don't complain. I told you it was simple. Well, if it's so simple, why don't you do it?

I've given lots of talks on "How to Be Outrageously Successful With the Opposite Sex". I've given the talks on cruise ships, to singles groups, to conventions, to seminar groups. Every time I've given the talk, the reactions I get to that statement are the same. The eyes roll and the women say: "Right, I'll do the asking" or "Me ask? What if he says no?" or "I could never get up the courage to do it".

OH, YOU'RE BREAKING MY HEART!

Now, let's define terms. When I say ask him out, I don't necessarily mean that you have to walk up to the guy and say: "Would you like to go out to dinner this Saturday?". If can you do that, great. It'll work lots of times. But if you can't do that, that's fine too. When I say "ask", I really mean <u>you should make a very clear indication that you have an interest</u>. Ask the guy to work out with you, or run with you when you jog, or give you a hand cooking or building something. Come on, you know what I'm talking about. Just do it! It works!!! Why? Well, that's where the male ego comes in.

Men have interesting egos. In fact, do you want to know a secret? The male ego will find it very hard to say no to <u>almost any woman who does the asking</u>. Here's why.

From day one of his dating life, the guy has done the asking. In the beginning it's nerve wracking. As time goes on, it becomes kind of fun. That wears off and it's just not as much fun as it used to be. In fact, at times it's no fun at all. Do you think we don't have that fear of rejection? Of course we do!!! But we know what we have to do to get what we want. So, we do it. Men would be thrilled to get a bit of a break from this. They would love to have the tables turned.

How many times do you think the average guy is asked out? Not often is right. So, when you do the asking, right away you're following one of the rules of being Outrageously Successful With the Opposite Sex. You're standing out from the crowd. You're not doing what everyone else is doing. <u>You are different</u>. Be as subtle or as direct as you want to be. Your chance of success is much higher than a guy's chance of success in asking a woman out. Don't believe me? Ask your male friends how they would feel if a woman asked them out. Then ask them how they would feel if a woman asked them out and offered to pay!

Now for some of the negative thoughts on this idea. I've heard them all! The first negative idea is that if a woman asks a man out, he'll think she's "easy". Doesn't she have a mind of her own? Can't she control her own situations? Are all men deranged rapists waiting to strike? (By the way, if you said "yes" to that last question, close this book and give it away. You're hopeless.) Can't the woman's thoughts about being thought of as "easy" be made clear right in the beginning? Take control of your own life.

The next objection is that women should <u>never</u> do the asking. It's a man's "job" to do all of the asking. You may well feel that way. But, if you want a cab, you can stand on the corner and wait for one to come to you, or you can wave one down. I know which one makes more sense. A lot of cabs could pass you by unless they know you have an <u>interest</u> in them. Many women have told me that they already do enough. They make it obvious that they have an interest in a man. Well, if that's obvious, I'd love to see subtle! It would take the C.I.A. to crack that code of "obvious" interest!

The best objection is: "What if he says 'no'?". Oh, you're breaking my heart again! Men have to put up with that all the time. They get more no's than yeses. In fact, they usually get a whole lot more no's than yeses. So what if he says no. Will you melt into brown sugar? Will he run a headline story in the morning newspaper telling the world he said "no" to you? Will he stand up in a crowded room & say: "Excuse me. Will everyone listen up. I'm going to turn this woman down." Don't be ridiculous.

FACE IT LADIES -- <u>YOU'RE CHICKEN!</u>

You're afraid and you don't want to admit it. You blow these smokescreen excuses hoping we'll buy it. We don't. You're not off the hook.

Oooo!!! That got some of you mad.

Good. Well, prove that I'm wrong!

Sneaky little devil, aren't I? I still love you...but you get the point, don't you?

What if he says yes? What a gold medal that would be for you! You got this relationship off the ground. If it weren't for you, there would BE no relationship. You would have walked away thinking about what it would have been like if he asked you out. You gave up control of the situation to him. Shame on you!

Another excuse women use has to do with a man feeling intimidated by a woman asking him out. Again, ladies, ask your male friends. Aside from those few "macho" guys who want to have everything under control, most men would be thrilled to have you make the first move. It just doesn't happen that often. So, when it does, it's met with as much pleasure as a winning lottery ticket.

Oh, stop being such cowards. Stop the excuses. <u>Just do it!</u>

You know that old story about the guy who goes up to every woman in a crowded room and asks them to sleep with him? Right. He gets his face slapped a lot, but he also wakes up with a lot of women. So it goes if you ask a lot of men to do something with you. You wind up doing a lot of great things with a lot of great men. Or with just one special one. It's your choice. What do you have to lose?

Chapter 15

SOME OF THE HOTTEST IDEAS EVER!

How about a chapter loaded with a bunch of ideas? I'll give you a little information about the ideas and let your imagination do the rest.

At an airport, how often do you get your seat assignment, board the plane and hope that you won't be sitting next to the person who just ate garlic and keeps clearing their sinuses? Or the person who seems set on getting you wrapped up in a conversation? Well, be a little outrageous and set yourself up better than that. Get to the terminal a little early and watch the people getting on line for seat assignments. When you see someone who looks interesting, get in line behind him or her. Wait until they get their seat assigned, then go to the clerk and ask for the seat next to that person. Who knows what could work out. Now, you negative people are saying: "He or she could be married or could be a jerk".

Well, that's typical negative thinking.

One thing's for sure: for the next few hours you have a captive audience and a lot of time to find out what's up. The worst that could happen is that nothing happens. What's the best thing that could happen? Well, you know! At least you don't have to smell garlic and listen to sinus problems for the whole flight!

I heard about one woman who waits for a rainy day and then goes out and hails a cab. She has the cabbie drive around town while she looks for interesting men who are hailing a taxi. When she finds one, she has the driver pull over and pick him up. She makes sure she's the first one to ask "Where are you going?". Don't you know that she's always going where the new passenger is going! What a coincidence. Another captive audience...and one who's grateful for being rescued from the rain.

- - -

Learn how to give a great backrub. While I was on vacation a while back, I took a class in massage. I walked into the class alone and was quickly paired up with a female partner. We learned fabulous backrub techniques. Most people think that all you do is have the person roll over and start to rub. No, no, no, no, no! Getting a great backrub is probably the closest thing to heaven that I can think of. It's relaxing, it's sexy and it's just plain fun. I only know of one person who doesn't melt at the thought of getting a great backrub. I've had a few thoughts about all his screws being tight anyway. Backrubs are a nice way of getting closer or getting together in the first place. They can be as intimate or as casual as you want. They're always a pleasure!

- - -

Lots of people say they're interested in going out and meeting people. But, then they go out and travel in herds...or should that be gaggles? It's tough enough approaching a stranger. Things are only made worse when there's an audience. Think about it.

A guy sees an interesting woman. She's been with four friends all night. The guy really wants to meet her, so he get his courage up and heads over to the waiting crowd. He starts talking to the lady and eventually steers in the direction of asking her out. Everyone knows it's coming. In fact, when he actually does the asking, there is dead silence while everyone listens. It's just like the commercial for that stockbroker. Whenever they talk, everyone listens. Believe me, it's the same way when a guy asks a woman in a group for a date. Her friends are all ears. Just the thought of that senario gives most men, including me, the shivers. If you're interested in having someone approach you, be alone for a while. If you're with a group of guys or girls, have them take a walk for a little while. Stand alone for a time. You'll be far more approachable than if you stay in the group. Most men would rather take on a Sumo wrestler than walk into a group of women and try to get a date with one of them.

If you'd like to increase your chances of being approached, sit alone and read a book. In fact, to make this a bit more effective, read this book! What a great lead in!!! Hold up the front cover so people can read the title. I don't know what more you could do to make it clear that you're approachable!

- - -

Men, I told the women that they have one technique they can use very successfully that you can't. Well, now it's time to even the score. Here's a technique that you can use that just won't work for women - borrow a baby.

I know you think you've heard this before, but I've never seen the second part of this idea written anywhere. Very simply, you have to really like kids. If you don't, you'll have a terrible time. And it'll show! So, if you don't love kids, move on to the next idea.

If you haven't moved on to the next idea, let's talk about where to get that baby. Think about your friends or relatives who have small children and offer to take them to a shopping mall. Usually, people are thrilled to have someone they trust take the baby for a while. It gives them a real breather.

Kids 3 years old or younger are the best. Women just love to see men alone with little children. It gives them good feelings about the man and it brings out their maternal instincts. And, believe it or not, kids can be a whole lot of fun! So, even if you don't meet anyone particularly interesting, you'll have a good time with the little kid.

- - -

Next idea. I've heard of people who hold elegant dinner parties and charge admission to the parties. The cost of the dinner party is usually substantial, ranging from $40 - $75 per dinner. The number of people invited is small. Perhaps there'll only be a dozen or two people at the affair, but often the parties will be well coordinated so that there's an even number of men and women.

Careful hosts or hostesses will even go so far as to screen the people by age group, education, interests and so forth. So, when you walk into one of these parties, you already know something about the people you'll be sharing the evening with. Poorly run parties simply invite people until all the seats are taken. There is really no regard for sex balance, age, interests or whatever.

The parties are run in people's homes, in restaurants or halls. The entertainment is most often simply the conversation of the people at the dinner. The advertising is simple, but the preparation for the dinners can be quite involved. What's to stop you from trying this idea in your area? Again, you might make a fair amount of money and you might meet some interesting people. You definitely will be putting yourself in the drivers seat, though!

- - -

To all you computer affectionados, you know that the term "computer dating" means two things. First, we all know it as the type of service which matches your application with the application of a member of the opposite sex. True computer dating operations use a computer. Others use humans, but are often still called computer dating.

The other type of computer dating, though, uses your own home computer. Across the nation, there are hundreds of what are called "bulletin boards". These are actually printed notices that appear on your computer monitor, just like the stock reports you're used to seeing on TV or in a brokers office. People use their computer to call the computer bulletin board and type in a message.

The message is then played back to anyone who calls the bulletin board, asking to see the messages currently on the board. The messages can range from selling a car to wishing Happy Birthday to someone. It didn't take people long to figure out that you can also put a personal ad on the bulletin board. In fact, some bulletin boards are just for personals.

Now, the bad news. Well over 90% of the ads on the bulletin boards are from men. This isn't bad news for women. The women can really do some shopping at home! When women put personals on the computer bulletin boards they're often inundated with responses.

How are the responses made? By electronic mail. A message is typed into the computer. It's then stored in what's actually a computer mail box. A computer will hold the message until the person who's to get the message calls for it with their computer. If you have no idea what I've been talking about, but it sounds interesting, ask for more information at your local computer shop. They'll certainly know about bulletin boards in your area and will help you get started. Isn't technology just amazing?

Chapter 16

76 GREAT IDEAS FOR MEETING
YOUR DREAM PERSON

So, you've read this far and you're convinced that there are better ways to meet singles than by standing in a bar, holding a drink, hoping for a miracle. But, you might say, where do I find these great people to try these great techniques on? Well, in this chapter, I'm going to give you a non-stop list of dozens of places to meet people. We all need our imaginations jogged at times - this list will do it for you:

- ❏ Volunteer organizations
- ❏ Travelling or in travel groups
- ❏ Auctions - before, during, after
- ❏ Churches, synagogues, etc.
- ❏ Political organizations
- ❏ Swimming pools or clubs
- ❏ Health clubs
- ❏ Museum shops
- ❏ Museums, themselves
- ❏ Cruises
- ❏ Restaurants
- ❏ Amateur theatre groups (men, this is a great one for you!!!)
- ❏ Professional theatre presentations
- ❏ Lectures
- ❏ Adult schools (teach a class or take one)
- ❏ While taking photographs in the park
- ❏ Weddings
- ❏ Jury duty
- ❏ Concerts
- ❏ Financial seminars
- ❏ Book sales
- ❏ Ticket lines
- ❏ Through friends
- ❏ Through relatives
- ❏ Wine & cheese tastings
- ❏ The racetrack
- ❏ The tennis courts
- ❏ Bowling
- ❏ Cooking classes

- ❑ Book shops
- ❑ Health fairs
- ❑ Car shows
- ❑ Boat shows
- ❑ Doctors office
- ❑ Art exhibits
- ❑ An organized nature walk
- ❑ Walking your dog
- ❑ Work
- ❑ Seminars
- ❑ Sales meetings
- ❑ Skating
- ❑ Flea markets
- ❑ Sporting events
- ❑ Biking
- ❑ Supermarket - the old standby - especially on Monday nights when most single people do their shopping.
- ❑ Camping
- ❑ Dances
- ❑ Dancing lessons
- ❑ Teaching dancing lessons!
- ❑ Resorts
- ❑ Civic organizations
- ❑ Fraternal organizations
- ❑ Conventions
- ❑ Post Office
- ❑ Dentist office
- ❑ Block parties
- ❑ Garage sales
- ❑ Libraries
- ❑ Zoos
- ❑ Amusement parks
- ❑ Bridge club
- ❑ Funerals!
- ❑ Beach
- ❑ Skiing
- ❑ On line at the bank
- ❑ Record shops
- ❑ Restaurants
- ❑ Church dinners
- ❑ Community projects or celebrations
- ❑ Ethnic organizations
- ❑ Exercise class
- ❑ Softball games
- ❑ Bus stops
- ❑ 4th of July celebrations

❑ Christmas parties
❑ Bird watching (yes, birdwatching!)

Want more? Look in your local newspaper, especially on Fridays when many papers have a special section for weekend events.

And the list goes on and on. In fact, I actually could have just put one word in this chapter and it would have told you where to meet people. ANYWHERE! Of course, anywhere. Just look around you. You're surrounded by people. You just have to decide to take the action to meet them. You have nothing to lose!

I can't let this list go by, however, without giving you more details about several of the suggestions I made.

Let's start at the top. My first suggestion was volunteer organizations. Like all of the other suggestions I've made in this book, volunteering should come from the heart. You shouldn't volunteer your time and talents with the idea of meeting a man or a woman. But don't be at all surprised if that's exactly what happens. In fact, I have a great story right along those lines. It'll illustrate several points I've been making.

I volunteer time to a local charitable organization. I've been working with them for about a year. Just a few weeks ago, I went to a meeting at the organization. When I walked in the door, my eyes almost popped out of my head. An absolutely gorgeous woman was standing across the room. Now, in the year that I'd been volunteering here, I hadn't met anyone I was even remotely interested in. But, as I said earlier, my purpose was to volunteer my time, not meet a woman.

Since we were both very busy for the entire time we were at the meeting, I didn't get much of a chance to talk with her. Fear not, all was not lost!

A few days later I spoke with the woman who was in charge of the organization. I'll call her Irene - because that's her name. I told Irene about the woman I met and asked if she knew anything about her. She told me that she only knew her name & her home phone number.

Only her name & home phone number!!! I was in heaven. She was as good as mine.

The next day I called her during the day, fully expecting (and hoping) to get an answering machine. She didn't let me down. Her answering machine picked up my call. When I heard the beep, I was center stage. Here's the message I left:

"Hi Carol, this is Paul...Paul...you remember, Paul Hartunian. We met on Sunday. Aw, come on, Carol, don't do this to me. You remember me, don't you (by now there was a clear whine in my voice). Well, anyway, I have an urgent message for you. I think it's urgent that you and I go out together. Now, if you agree, call 1-900-DATE PAUL. There will be a charge of $2.00 for the first minute and $1.00 for every additional minute. Well, if you don't want to do that, you can call me at my home number which is --------.

"Unacceptable excuses for not going out with me are: I already have a boyfriend, I've just been transferred to Saudi Arabia or any excuse having to do with washing your hair. The only acceptable excuse is: my ex-husband is wanted by the FBI for killing my last six boyfriends. So, assuming that none of the previous excuses are in the way, I'll look forward to hearing from you." I hung up.

Within mere hours, the phone rang. Jackpot. The dream woman was mine.

Was this an insane message to leave a total stranger? Sure. But what did I have to lose. Her? I didn't think so. I really thought that she'ld see the humor in the message and respond, which she did. And what a real charge it gave the beginning of our relationship. None of the same old "How about dinner and a movie? (yawn)."

So, what are the lessons here?

Correct. #1) You never know where you are going to find a delightful match and #2) stand out from the crowd. Be different. Be daring.

"NO GUTS, NO GLORY!"

Now let's go down the list a bit. How about those health clubs. First, let me say that I think that health clubs are grossly overrated as places to meet the opposite sex. At least the ones I've gone to were no thrill. Sure, the women looked great (make that sensational). But, they were far from friendly.

It's the same old thing we've been talking about. Men want women. Women want men. But still, both sexes put on scowling faces that would drive anyone away. And then they wonder why no one approaches them.

Now that I've given my opinion that health clubs are overrrated, I'll follow-up by saying that I think they're still good places to meet. Not great, mind you - good. If you can get past that hard exterior that lots of people seem to carry around with them, you'll probably do very well in health clubs. You're pretty much captive in the club for an hour or two. Especially if you're riding a stationary bike next to someone. Use that time. Lots of times it just takes one word - "Hi" - to melt away the steely outer coating of the person on the next bike. If not, what did you lose? You weren't talking to them anyway!

You've got to admit that in health clubs there's not much a person can hide...at least about their bodies. So, what you see is what you get. It's up to you to see what's on the inside of this person. That's what the time on the bike is for!

Further on down the list I mention cruises. I work for a number of cruise lines. I'm hired to give seminars on self-improvement for the passengers. They're very light and entertaining and lots of people attend. I give three seminars a week and each seminar has more people than the previous one.

OK, it's your turn again. Tell me how I'm benefiting by this.

If you said that I'm in the power position, which women find very attractive - you're absolutely right. You've been paying attention.

But, you say, "That's fine for you, but what about me. I'm not giving any seminars. If I took a cruise, I'd be a passenger."

Let's talk about cruises. I'm sure you've seen The Love Boat TV show at least once. Well, real cruises aren't <u>exactly</u> like that. But they sure are close! I've been on dozens of cruises and I've almost always seen the same thing. The passengers are a diverse group. There are lots of single people, lots of married people, old, young, in between. As the passengers are boarding the ship on the first day, everyone's in a group. That night, it's like the old high school dances - the women stay to one side of the ship and the men to the other.

But then, the magnetism takes over. It's not long before you see fewer and fewer single sex groups. You see more and more newly found couples holding hands. By the end of the cruise, you see very few groups of either men or women walking off the ship. New romances have popped up all over.

Dollar for dollar I think cruises are one of the best vacation values around. If you've never been on a cruise, don't roll your eyes. I always have people telling me that if they ever went on a cruise, they'd be bored to death, they'd get claustrophobic, they'd get sea sick and so on. If you have been on a cruise, you know this just isn't true. On the cruises I've gone on, there wasn't enough time to do all that was offered. Seasickness wasn't even a point of discussion.

Some ships are so beautiful you think you're in a palace. As for you just being part of a crowd - haven't we covered that? Let me tell you - from personal experience - that cruises are great places to showboat. If you have any talents at all you'll get chance after chance to be in the spotlight. Even if you think you have no talents, you'll still have lots of shots at the spotlight.

So, if you've been thinking about a cruise but just have never done it, now's the time. (I sound like a travel agent, don't I?).

Next - amateur theatre groups. In parentheses I indicated that they are especially good for men. That's the understatement of the year!!!

About two years ago I got the urge to try my hand at acting. So, I looked in the local paper and saw that the theatre group in town was holding auditions for a play. I went.

Have you ever walked into a room and had everyone turn and look at you? If you're a man, the first thing you do is check your zipper (women, what do you check?). Well, that's exactly what happened to me. I had no idea why they were staring at me...and no one would tell me. I went through the audition and got the lead role in the play! Now that wasn't too hard.

During rehearsals, the facts of this case started to come out. It seems that there is a great - no make that tremendous - lack of men in theatre. Yes, from the top to the bottom. From the little community theatre to the major productions. Men are a rare commodity. If a man walks in the door of many theatres and he's still breathing, he gets just about anything he wants.

Well, here we go again. I was out doing something that interested me and it turned out to be a double jackpot. Here I was in a setting where men were rare, women were in abundance and I had the lead role (translate that into the term "power position" - does that term sound familiar?). A no lose situation.

Women, I'm sorry, but it just isn't a great place for you to meet men. There are just too many women.

Let's move on and talk about adult school classes. We've already talked about taking classes. Another double winner - you learn something you enjoy and you just might find someone you'd like to spend time with outside of class. But once again, let's think on a bit of a higher plane. How about teaching the class?

Think of all the benefits. You get to teach something you enjoy. You get paid, and... and... RIGHT! <u>You're in the power position.</u> You are standing out from all of the students because <u>you</u> are the teacher. A triple win. Life's a ball, isn't it?

A little further down the list I mention jury duty. Fat chance, eh? Oh yeah! (Here comes another story!).

During my research for this book I spoke to a man who had bad news turn into good. The bad news - he got a notice to serve on jury duty. The good news - a very attractive woman was on the same jury. The better news - she was the forewoman. The best news - they were locked up (along with the rest of the jurors) for four days, deliberating the case. At the end of the four days, the defendant got a not guilty verdict and the man got a date. A double win if I ever heard one! Even jury duty can be good news.

Move down the list a bit to where I've listed "Dances, Dancing lessons, Teaching dancing lessons". If they just seem like three more ideas on this list, you haven't been paying attention.

THIS IS A PERFECT EXAMPLE OF
A PROGRESSION OF POWER!

First, let's look at dances. You walk into the dance and you immediately become one of hundreds of people. If you're a great dancer, you can stand out. But, aside from that, you're doing battle with everyone else there. Poor choice.

How about dance lessons? You've certainly narrowed down the odds, since there are only a dozen or so people in most dance classes. A better choice, but you're still one of a number.

Teaching dance lessons - now you're talking! <u>You are the teacher.</u> You're in the power position. You're competing against absolutely no one. You stand alone. This, of course, is the best choice.

OK. So you can't dance. Or you don't want to dance. Just change that to what you want to do. You can do it! Take lessons or teach lessons. The progression of power.

I could go on forever giving you thoughts on every one of the ideas I've listed in the previous chapter. But, that's your homework. Don't just go down the list and say: "volunteer organization, travel, auctions, churches, political organizations - none of them will work for me." Quite to the contrary. Your job is to go down that list and think about at least one or two ways each and every one of those suggestions can work for you - because they all can.

Treat this assignment as a test. You have to test your knowledge of what you've already read in this book. If you can't think of one or two ways each of those suggestions can be put to work for you, you haven't been paying attention. Go back and start the book again if you have to. I've given you dozens - maybe hundreds - of ideas. Just put some of them to work!

Chapter 17

AN INCREDIBLE FREE OFFER

To close off this section, I'd like to tell you about an offer I'm sure you'll like. It's cute, fun...and free.

In 1981, I was having dinner with a friend. We were talking about anything that came to mind. It was one of those nights where we were out to change the world. You know what I mean. We were going to solve all of the world's problems.

Well, the discussion got around to singles meeting each other. We were talking about the typical ways singles try to meet. We were talking about the little success many singles were having. We came to the brilliant conclusion that there must be a better way.

One of my genius ideas was to have everyone's eyes genetically engineered so that they would change color at a certain time. So, if you approached a person you were interested in, your eyes would turn green. If you had a casual interest, but weren't quite sure, they would turn yellow. If you had no interest at all, they would turn red. The other person's eyes would also change colors, depending on their interest in you. The best part of this idea is that you would have no control over the color your eyes changed and you could not see what color your eyes were changing to! So, if you walked up to someone and your eyes turned green and so did theirs, you're set. If not, no damage done. Not a bad idea, eh? Well, thanks for giving me a few minutes to try out that brilliant idea on you.

Anyway, as my friend and I were talking, I took out a pen and wrote some words on a napkin. The words were: "I've been carrying this card for a long time hoping to meet someone like you. Bars and pick-up lines are just not my style. So, I hope to meet you using this card. I'd really like to find out who you are and tell you exactly what it was about you that attracted me. My name and phone number are on the back of this card. The option of calling will be yours. But, I'll really be sorry if you don't call. Let's spend some time together. Please call and let me know who you are!".

"What if these words were printed on a business card? A person could write their name on the back of the card, hand it to someone or have it passed to them, and walk away, without even having to talk to them!", I asked out loud.

It sounded like a curious idea, so I had 1,000 cards printed up. I kept a few to try myself and gave the rest to my single friends. I asked them to give them a try and let me know how they worked out.

The response was tremendous! People loved them. They were great for shy people, for people who like to clown around, for people who want to just have fun with them. They worked for everybody!

I called that first card the "Introduction Card" for obvious reasons. It took me about a half-hour to design four other cards. One card is called a "Hug Card". It says: "FREE HUG! This card entitles the holder to one hug from any consenting man, woman or child."

The next card is called the "Snuggle Certificate" and says: "SNUGGLE CERTIFICATE - This certificate is good for one long, warm snuggle with a person of the holder's choice".

Then there's the "Kiss Coupon". It says: "Kiss Coupon! This coupon can be exchanged for one, big juicy kiss from anyone who'll enjoy it".

The final card in the set is the "Intimacy Card" and it says: "INTIMACY CARD! This card can be redeemed for one intimacy of the holder's choice with any consenting adult".

I had some of each of these cards printed up and again gave them away to friends. In no time at all, they were back for more, so I knew I had something good. Now, what to do with these cards.

For a while I gave some thought to selling them, but that idea died. Actually, I was having such a good time giving them away, I decided to keep on doing just that. I wrote to a few newspapers and radio shows. I sent them samples of the cards. I also told them that I would give away sets of these, at no charge. All people would have to do is send a stamped, self-addressed envelope for each set they wanted. There would be no strings attached. The phone started ringing off the hook. The reporters wanted to know why I was doing this, what I had to gain, how I was going to make money on this. "What's the catch?", they asked.

There was no catch, and there still isn't. Since I first started giving these cards away in 1981, I've given away countless tens of thousands every Valentine's Day. In fact, a few weeks before Valentine's Day, the radio and newspaper reporters start to mention the story again. Just before Valentine's

Day, I usually get 1,000 letters a day (that's right, <u>one thousand letters a day</u>!), each asking for some cards, which I've since called "Lovenotes".

I get lots of letters telling me how people are using the Lovenotes. There are no rules. Your imagination is your only limitation on how you can use them. People were slipping Hug cards into their husband's wallets or briefcases so they would find them when they got to work. People were using the introduction cards in dozens of different ways to meet people. Intimacy cards were found on pillows. Kiss cards were being taped to bathroom mirrors. Kids were giving Hug cards to their parents and parents were giving them to their kids. In fact, one guy was using the Intimacy cards to meet people, instead of using the Introduction card. That's not exactly what I had in mind when I designed them, but who am I to object? Lovenotes were, and are, being used by both married and single people, men & women, very young and very old.

So, the bottom line to this rather lengthy introduction to Lovenotes, is that I'd like you to have some. I've reproduced a set of cards here. They are full size. Notice that they are protected by a federal copyright. So, they can't be copied without my permission. Well, <u>you have my permission to copy a few sets for your own personal use.</u> I'm not granting permission to reproduce them in large quantities or to sell them. Only a few sets for your own personal use. But that should be plenty.

When you have the cards reproduced you also must have the copyright notice reproduced on them as well. Use them to your heart's - and imagination's - content. And if you think of some ingenious new ways to use them, especially to meet other singles, let me know! They can be a lot of fun and they could be just what you need to meet that person who hits the jackpot with you. Anyway, what do you have to lose?

Kiss Coupon!

*THIS COUPON CAN BE
EXCHANGED FOR ONE, BIG
JUICY KISS FROM ANYONE
WHO'LL ENJOY IT.*

© 1981 LoveNotes

SNUGGLE CERTIFICATE

THIS CERTIFICATE IS GOOD
FOR ONE LONG, WARM SNUGGLE
WITH A PERSON OF THE
HOLDER'S CHOICE.

© 1981 LoveNotes

I'VE BEEN CARRYING THIS CARD FOR A LONG
TIME HOPING TO MEET SOMEONE LIKE YOU.
BARS & PICK-UP LINES ARE JUST NOT MY
STYLE. SO I HOPE TO MEET YOU USING THIS
CARD. I'D REALLY LIKE TO FIND OUT WHO YOU
ARE AND TELL YOU EXACTLY WHAT IT WAS
ABOUT YOU THAT ATTRACTED ME. MY FIRST NAME &
PHONE NUMBER ARE ON THE BACK OF THIS
CARD. THE OPTION OF CALLING WILL BE
YOURS. BUT I'LL REALLY BE SORRY IF YOU
DON'T CALL. LET'S SPEND SOME TIME
TOGETHER. PLEASE CALL AND LET ME KNOW
WHO YOU ARE!

© 1981 LoveNotes

FREE HUG!

THIS CARD ENTITLES
THE HOLDER TO ONE HUG
FROM ANY CONSENTING MAN,
WOMAN OR CHILD.

© 1981 LoveNotes

INTIMACY CARD!

THIS CARD CAN BE REDEEMED

FOR ONE INTIMACY OF THE

HOLDER'S CHOICE WITH ANY

CONSENTING ADULT.

© 1981 LoveNotes

Chapter 18

WHERE HAS ALL THE ROMANCE GONE?

Where has the romance gone, indeed! Have you ever heard that question before? Maybe only on TV or in the newspapers. Hopefully not in a relationship you've been involved in.

Up to now, we've only been talking about how to meet that special man or woman. How about a little bit on how to keep the romance in you relationship? If we're going to talk about keeping them, we have to talk about romance.

When most people talk about relationships that have gone bad, romance is often at the bottom of the problem. The romance is gone. One of the problems is that men & women have different definitions of romance. Let's talk about it.

It's no secret that sex and romance are tied together. But men and women see the tie in <u>very</u> different ways. Women say "Give me romance and I'll give you sex." Men say, "Give me sex and I'll give you romance." So, we have a stand-off. Many times, neither side will "give in" and give the other person what they want first. So, hostility starts to grow.

What do you do?

The answer is really fairly simple. Actually, maybe a bit too simple. But, this works...

It seems that the way to approach a relationship is to think like the other person. Men should think like women and women should think like men.

THE GOLDEN RULE IS WRONG!

Don't treat others the way <u>you</u> want to be treated. Treat people the way <u>they</u> want to be treated.

That's it!

Men - instead of going into a relationship with thoughts of what you want, why not go in thinking about what she wants. Women, do the same. Think like a man!

Now stop making those faces. It's not going to kill you. It just may provide you with lots of benefits.

So many times we've heard about the "me-first" society - the "me generation". That has to be abandoned when you go into a relationship. "Me-first" just doesn't work in a relationship. If it does, it's not a relationship.

Women, do you know what's virtually at the top of the list of things men hate?

Shopping!

So, think like a man. Do you really think he wants to go shopping with you? Right, he doesn't. He doesn't slump into the chairs in the clothes store and frown because he's having a great time. So, go with your friends.

Men, how interested do you think women are in sitting on the couch all day watching football. I can assure you it's not high on their list.

If we would only think more like the person we are trying to please, life would be so much easier. Sure, it's going to be hard at the beginning. We're used to having our own way. We're so used to being selfish - to some degree or other - that it's a hard habit to break. But break it. The rewards are great.

Now don't get me wrong. Men, don't volunteer to go shopping if you really hate it (I'd rather have a root canal done). Women, don't start showing an interest in football if it's not genuine. But there are lots of things you can do. Spend a little time rubbing each others backs. Or a little more time with the lights low. Or maybe a little more time in front of the mirror when you get ready to go out. Look hot. It pays.

Stop worrying about money. You're probably exaggerating the problem. Enjoy yourselves.

Flowers go a long way - and I mean both of you!

Tell your partner how good he or she looks. Compliment a good job or a good idea or a kind gesture.

Spend some time thinking like your partner thinks. What do they like? What annoys them? What are they missing? What thrills them? I don't just mean what excites them. I mean what thrills them. You don't want to keep them "happy". You want them thrilled.

Well, do it. Thrill them!

Money is meant to be spent. Hearts are meant to give. Do it.

SECTION 2

THE MISTAKES

What's all the big commotion about dating? You just do it, don't you? I mean you meet someone, you make a date and you go out? Isn't that right? Isn't it?

Well, it just doesn't seem to be that easy. Let's not get too philosophical about this. Let's just agree that it doesn't seem to work out that easily and let's get to work on correcting it.

So, what happens to screw up the works? Actually, lots of things. In this section, I'd like to go over the "10 Biggest Dating Mistakes People Make and How to Avoid Them". I'll tell you what they are and I'll tell you how to avoid them - or how to stop doing them! I'll also tell you which of the 10 is the biggest mistake and why. This one's a real killer!

Let's go!

Chapter 19

BIG MISTAKE #1

The first of "The Big 10" is that people are not excited and they're not exciting. I mean lots of people are not excited about ANYTHING from man landing on the moon to just being alive! You practically have to throw them a hand grenade to get a reaction from them. How someone can't be excited about being alive is beyond me.

We're living in the most exciting time ever.

Think about even the seemingly smallest things in life. For instance, I was recently in London. While I was there, I had breakfast with a friend. That same evening I had dinner at my home in New Jersey. Doesn't that amaze you just a little bit? Very simply, if you don't find life exciting, I'm not going to be able to help you. Life IS exciting and the more you enjoy that excitement, the more you will show it. The more you show it, the more people will feel excitement radiating from you.

Imagine this first date. You're out with someone you don't know. You're both a little nervous and a little excited. You want to get a nice flow of conversation going, so you ask about the other person's job.

"How do you like your job?" is your question.

"Oh, it's OK I guess" is the lackluster reply.

You follow up with "How was your last vacation?".

"It was fair" are the words you get back.

"Do you like this car?".

"It'll do".

"Did you like the movie?".

"It wasn't bad".

"Well how do you like your heartbeat, for God's sake. You have to be excited about the fact that it's still beating, don't you?".

"Yeah, but heart attack IS the number 1 killer in this country, you know".

Now how many times are you going to want to go out with this character. I mean the fireworks at the birthday celebration of the Statue of Liberty would leave a clown like this cold!

Excitement adds spice not only to a relationship, but to you!

EXCITED PEOPLE ARE EXCITING PEOPLE

Exciting people attract other people. They make other people excited. Now, keep in mind that I'm not talking about the giddy, giggly space cadets that find everything "just awesome". I'm talking about people who are excited about being alive.

Everyone wants excitement in their lives. That's why so many people watch the daytime and nighttime soap operas. To many people, the soaps are exciting! In fact, lots of people live parts of their lives through the soaps. They don't feel that their lives can be exciting, so they depend on the soaps for thrills. Not only are these people not excited, they are not exciting.

What does it take to be exciting? Do you have to be a Space Shuttle astronaut or an Olympic athlete or a movie star? Of course not. All it takes is a real feeling of thrill in whatever it is you enjoy or whatever you are good at. Some time ago, I was speaking with a guy whose real passion in life was table tennis. Yes, ping pong! When he first started talking, I had to fight back the urge to roll my eyes up toward the ceiling. Really, how interesting can ping pong be? You know, it didn't take very long for his enthusiasm to rub off on me. Now, mind you, I haven't become a big fan of ping pong, but I can say I look at it a little differently now that I felt the enthusiasm he had for the game.

ENTHUSIASM IS VERY CONTAGIOUS.

If you are anywhere near it, you can catch it very easily. It just takes you over. Remember those pep rallies from high school, or a political rally or a great concert? You may not have been enthusiastic when you first got to the event, but it didn't take very long for you to catch the enthusiasm that was circulating among the crowd. It was electrifying. Remember?

Unfortunately, there is a quick cure for enthusiasm. It's faster and more effective than any vaccine known to man. Curiously, it's the cure for enthusiasm, but it's the cause of a far more serious problem. It's boredom - routine - depression - the blues, whatever you want to call it. It strikes quickly and it can be deadly.

How do we combat the problem? It's really not very hard. In fact, nothing in this book is very hard - if you just do it!

What's exciting to you? Is it astronomy, cooking, biking, business? Are you REALLY excited about it or do you just like it? If you're really excited about it, talk about it! I'm not saying that you should become an evangelist. I mean when the opportunity comes up, talk about your interest. Really feel the excitement you feel when you are doing it. Let your excitement show in your eyes, your words, your actions.

If you can't think of anything you really love, think about something you simply like. The next time you do it, fake some real enthusiasm. If you're playing racquetball, next time you hit a great kill shot and score a point, give a good "YEAH" and clap your hands together. You may be surprised at how quickly you're getting a real thrill out of what you are doing.

Think of something you're good at. Now don't tell me you're not good at anything. Everybody is good at something. Just think about one thing you are really good at. Again, I don't care what it is. You can be really good at getting mildew off of bathroom tiles, for all it matters. The point is that you have to feel some real thrill for what you're good at. Realize that most of the people are terrible at what you are a pro at. Ask me to speak in front of a large group of people and I'm a pro. Ask me to sew a rip in my jeans and I'm a boob.

Lots of people live in a rut. They go to the same job, take the same train, eat the same lunch, read the same newspaper and on and on. They lose that zest for life. They lose that excitement...and it shows. It shows in the expression on their faces, the tone of their voices and the frequency of their complaints. They're appealing.

Curiously, though, it's this very group of people who have the greatest demands. They're only interested in dating gorgeous, exciting, go-for-it people. They only want the cream of the crop. What they really want is someone to make a new life for them. Obviously, it's just not going to happen, but they keep on hoping. They always believe that miracles can happen.

IF YOU WANT EXCITEMENT,
YOU'VE GOT TO PROVIDE EXCITEMENT

Become excited about something - almost anything. But really feel it. Don't fake it. <u>Phony excitement is just as easy to spot as no excitement.</u> Don't be happy just surviving in life. Really thrive!

Chapter 20

BIG MISTAKE #2

People have tunnel-vision. They're narrow thinkers. They don't try a variety of things. They don't try different ways of meet people or places to go on a first date. They don't test different foods or types of friends. You already know that old cornball about "variety being the spice of life". Well, it's also the "spice" of dating.

We all know lots of ways to do a particular task. If I asked you to get me change for a dollar, you could go to the bank and get change. You could also go to a candy store, or a change machine, or your pocket. You could ask someone else to do it. There are lots of ways to accomplish whatever you want to do.

For some reason, when it comes to dating, variety seems to be put on hold for many people. If I were to ask you what the typical first date is, many of you would say dinner and/or a movie, right? Actually, I couldn't think of a more boring first date. Why? <u>Because it's so typical!</u> It shows no imagination, no excitement. In fact, almost anything is better than a dinner and movie first date.

As for meeting people, most of us have ways which we continue to use, <u>whether they work or not.</u>

IF YOU DO WHAT YOU'VE ALWAYS DONE, YOU GET THE SAME RESULTS YOU'VE ALWAYS GOTTEN!

The bars are still packed to capacity on Friday nights, even though one of the leading topics of discussion among singles is how terrible the bars are! If they are so terrible, why do people still go?

Because they're used to them.

It's the way they've always done things. It's the way many people will continue to do things.

Think about what you do in your dating life. Start right at the very beginning. How do you meet people? Do you use at least 10 different ways? Do you use them all or do you have two or three favorites that you keep going back to? Well, unless you have at least 10 different ways of meeting people and you use them all, you're not even coming close to using all that you have available to you.

How about the places you go on a date. Do you have at least 30 different places to go or things to do? If not, why not?

How about "nice, warm things" to say to your date. Do you have at least 30 of them? If not, you're in trouble. Saying "You're really nice to be with" or "I really feel comfortable with you" just is not enough. You need a warehouse of things to say. Again, <u>sincerity</u> is the key word here. I don't want you coming up with a bunch of meaningless lines. But variety is exciting.

I heard of a terrific idea concerning places to go on a date. One person keeps a little notebook of dating ideas. As a good idea comes up in the paper, or in a conversation, the idea goes into the dating ideas book. Then, when it's time to come up with ideas for places to go or things to do, out comes the dating ideas book and the job is a snap.

The moral of this chapter is:

"Different is exciting - routine is boring"

Be exciting.

Chapter 21

BIG MISTAKE #3

The 3rd biggest dating mistake people make is that they're afraid to experiment. Now this is not the same as mistake #2, which was not trying variety. Variety is using a number of things which you've tried or done before in a rotation. Experimentation, though, is trying something you've never done before. This can be as simple as flying a kite.

Lots of people get tied up on this one for a variety of reasons. Sometimes it's the fear of failure. People don't want to try new things because they're afraid they'll fail. Well, you're not going to get a lot of sympathy from me on this one. The people who are not afraid to fail are the ones who get the real thrills out of life.

NO GUTS, NO GLORY!

It's funny, but the people who aren't afraid to fail are the ones who find that many times there isn't even anything to fear (Here's that fear again!). They went out and tried something only to find that it wasn't even possible to fail. So, they're out there having a ball while the rest of the people are at the starting line, still afraid to take the first step.

I was on a cruise just a short time ago. I was sitting by the pool when a 3 year old little girl and her mother came to the edge of the pool. Mom was putting a pair of swimmies on the little girl's arms. The little girl couldn't wait for Mom get done. She kept saying "Come on, Mom. I want to get into the water". As this was going on, people all around were commenting on how cold the water in the pool was. In fact, Mom even said something to the little girl about the water being cold. Well, those words went right in one ear and out the other.

Finally, Mom was done with the swimmies. The little girl rocketed into the pool like her bathing suit was on fire. As soon as she got in, she yelled out "It's not cold, Mommy. Come on in!". Mom put one toe in and found out she was right. It wasn't cold! The other people who were complaining about the water hadn't even been in!! They were afraid of the water being cold just by looking at it! Leave it to little kids. They don't know the meaning of fear.

Another bit of defeatist thinking people waste their time on is the idea of "shouldn't". Such as, "I really <u>shouldn't</u> do that at my age". Or, "I <u>shouldn't</u> be seen doing that. What if some of my associates come by?". Oh, nonsense.

PROBABLY THE ONLY THING YOU SHOULDN'T BE DOING IS THINKING YOU SHOULDN'T BE DOING SOMETHING

Again, be reasonable. No, you shouldn't cause damage or injury. No, you shouldn't cause insult. But your mother taught you all of that already. I don't have to repeat it, do I?

I'll give you one break, though. If you don't want to experiment on the first date, I'll let you slide by with that one. A good argument can be made for the idea that a first date should be interesting and exciting, but since you both will be nervous enough, adding another factor like experimenting with something new, might not be a thrill to some people.

By the way, if you think any of this is only directed toward men, think again. Women, I'm talking to you too. You have half the responsibility for the date - and later, the relationship - being successful.

For those of you who want to experiment even on the first date, though, you'll get a standing ovation from me. We're in the same corner.

Whenever you get a chance, experiment. Who knows, if you don't try it now, you may never get another opportunity. Anyway, experimentation leaves memories and you want to be responsible for lots of memories.

Chapter 22

BIG MISTAKE #4

Have you ever heard of guys who rent a limo, buy a dozen long stemmed roses and go to the poshest restaurant in town on a first date - all to impress the girl? Well, they're guilty of the 4th mistake in the Big 10. They go way overboard on a first date, just to make a good impression. I really don't have a good example of how women go overboard on a first date, since it is so rare that they are responsible for first dates. Actually, that's a shame. But, we'll get to that later.

I recently read a book on dating in which the author suggested that you really let it roll on the first date. Let money be just about no object. Don't spare any expense in putting together a real dazzler of a first date. The author's idea was that if you're lavish on a first date, there is almost certainly going to be a second date.

Is this guy serious? First dates are for getting acquainted. First dates are certainly for making an impression, but not the wrong one. If you come up with a dazzling first date, what do you follow up with?

A few years back, a friend of mine was dying to date this one girl. He was going through all the usual strategies, in his head mind you, to get the date. He forgot one strategy.

HE DIDN'T ASK HER!

Once he got past that hurdle, he found out how easy it really was to get the date. Now he had the problem of thinking about where to go and what to do.

He wanted to make a good impression, so everything had to be right. He went top of the line on this date. First, he rented a limo. Then he made dinner reservations at an exclusive club which was over 90 minutes away. Everything at dinner was first class. He had the limo waiting to take them home when they were finished.

Sounds great, doesn't it? So what was the problem. The problem was that he really hadn't spent much time talking to this girl before they went out. He just asked her out and let price be no object. There's no doubt that it was a spectacular evening, but what was he going to follow it up with? What was the second date going to be like? Well, knowing what he spent on the first date, the second date probably wasn't going to go much beyond a few burgers at a fast food place.

Where did my friend go wrong? He set up a scene that was going to be hard to duplicate later in the relationship - if the relationship continued. It would have been very reasonable for the girl to think that he was really a high roller and that the good times were going to continue to roll. When they didn't, she probably had the right to be disappointed, even annoyed. He was just setting up the glamorous scene to make that first big impression, but it was the wrong one.

Now, understand me. I don't see anything wrong with putting together an expensive, dazzling night out. There's no doubt they are fun times. But not on a first date. Save the dazzling times for something special - an anniversary, a special accomplishment or even sometime when you just want to show someone you care for them. You already have something going with this person, so the splash will have meaning.

What do I suggest for a first date? Actually, I suggest just the opposite of what my friend did. Something very inexpensive, something that will give you a chance to be together for a while without lots of pressure. Don't you think that my friends dazzling date was a real pressure situation? For him, the pressure was the cost and what the girl was thinking about him and the date. For her, the pressure was "Now, what do I have to do for all of this?". Not a real pleasant scene for a first date.

On a first date, get to know someone. Don't want to have to worry about a dozen things. Feel comfortable and get your date to feel comfortable.

On Fridays, my local paper has a few pages of listings of what is going on in the area. Every Friday, there are dozens of listings of things that are free or just about free. Your paper has something similar. Look for something that you will both enjoy and that will give you time to talk and maybe walk a bit.

DON'T PICK A MOVIE!

All you are going to do is sit there for two hours, feeling uncomfortable. You're only delaying the inevitable. You're going to have to talk to each other. If you're comfortable, you're going to hold hands and even kiss! Get started early.

Have a sense of humor. So many first dates are <u>so serious</u>! There's lots of planning, lots of detail, lots of going overboard. Why not go to the juggling demonstration at the local college? Or the street fair being held? Or bike riding? Or take paddle boats out on the lake? Would you like me to continue? OK. Why not go to the airport? Or how about a comedy club -- now there's a great idea.

Everyone, both male and female, wants their date to laugh. Maybe you can't tell jokes very well. Then, leave it to the pros. During the comedy club routines, you can do a little talking and lots of laughing. When I go to comedy clubs I generally leave holding my sides. So, the pros set up the rest of the night for you. You both leave laughing and then, of course, you spend some time retelling the jokes to each other and laughing some more. What a great first date.

Whatever you do, don't make the deadly mistake of planning something serious and somber. Going to a lecture on the devastation which would be created by a nuclear war is not my idea of a fun first date. I can't see many laughs popping up at that lecture. Remember:

KEEP IT LIGHT!

That means keep the atmosphere light and funny and do things which are casual. Save the dazzle for something special. It will mean a whole lot more.

HOW TO FLIRT

Susan G. Rabin, M.A.

Counselor • Health and Human Sexuality • Lecturer

*Are you flirting, dating and relating the way you want to?
Improve your social and sexual survival skills for the 90's. Learn
from this outstanding audio cassette and let Susan Rabin, M.A.
noted sexologist and media personality give you permission to flirt
and enjoy it!*

Finally on Audio Cassette

as an outgrowth of her popular class at The Discovery Center:

How to Flirt, Date AND MEET YOUR MATE

Explore with Susan:
** 3 essential flirting skills *What to say after "hello *Being
an "active" listener *Dealing with rejection*Interpersonal
communication skills *Reading non-verbal signals*

*To order send check for $13.95 to: Ultimate Secrets,
P.O.Box 43033, Upper Montclair, N.J. 07043*

Chapter 23

BIG MISTAKE #5

Why do you want to date? Why do you want to be with a man or woman? Sounds like an obvious question, doesn't it? Well, it's not. Lots of people never focus on <u>why</u> they're dating in the first place. They don't know why they're dating in general and they even don't know why they're dating a particular person. How many times have you heard someone say "I don't know why I went out with him (or her). We had nothing in common. I knew that I really wasn't interested, but I went anyway."?

"Come on", you're saying. "I'm dating for sex.". Well, now that you said that, thousands of people just said, "Wait a minute, I'm not dating for sex. I'm dating to find someone to marry." Or, "I'm dating for companionship", or whatever the reason is. Lots of people never focus in on what they want from a dating relationship. They'll let the relationship wander and they'll take what comes their way. Or, they may be afraid to say what's on their mind. The woman may be uncomfortable saying that she doesn't want sex. The man may be uncomfortable saying that he is looking for someone to marry. So, the relationship meanders.

Focus in on what you want, on your feelings, desires, your likes and dislikes. Where do you want to go with all of this? Are you going to decide or are you going to let the other person decide it all? If you let the other person decide, what if he or she has also made the same decision - they're going to let YOU decide. Now you're in a fine situation. No one is deciding.

You have to take responsibility for your own life and that includes your dating life. I'm sure you've heard people say "What do you like to do?" and the other person says "Oh, anything is fine". OK, then let's get dressed up as chickens and throw eggs at cars in Times Square!

No one likes to do ANYTHING! I don't want to go out to dinner and eat liver or squid or any of that other non-human food. I don't want to go to the opera. I don't want to go bowling. Now there is nothing wrong with any of these things. They're just not for me. I want to go rock climbing. I want to go sailing. I want to get as many great backrubs as I can. So, if you want to eat liver while you bowl, it's not going to be with me. I'll make some other suggestions, but liver and bowling are out.

You have to make the same decisions. There are stacks of people who've let years go by without making decisions. "I didn't think you wanted to sleep with me", "I thought you wanted me to date other people", "I didn't know you hated going to the opera with me" are all too familiar. What do YOU want? Make the decision and don't be afraid to talk about it.

What's the worst that could happen? Right, the person you could be dating could end the relationship. But what kind of relationship did you have when you were always doing things you didn't want to do? It was a desperate relationship. It was one of those "Well, it's better than nothing" relationships. It wasn't better than nothing.

It was worse than nothing!

You were just becoming what your date wanted you to become.

YOU WEREN'T YOU ANYMORE!

As flattering as it may sound, people really don't want clones of themselves walking around this earth. They certainly don't want to date their clone. It would drive anybody mad!

Don't be afraid to stop in the middle of a relationship and say "Where are we going with this relationship? What are we doing? What do we each want?" Relationships have a tendency to wander aimlessly. Many times this is because the people involved in the relationship are afraid to say "STOP! What's going on here?". They're afraid of what they may hear. So, they'd rather suffer silently than take the shot at the gold medal. After all, you might not get any medal at all, right? So, you might as well be happy with an honorable mention. It's boring, but it's something. Forget it. It's boring and it's nothing.

Finally, think about whether you want to be trendy or not. Lots of people follow trends and give up a good part of their own decision making. If one of the so-called authorities wakes up one morning and decides that your favorite fashion, or your favorite eyeliner or your favorite restaurant is out, does that mean that it's true? Again, I want to know what YOU want, not what someone else wants. Do you love clam digger pants? Do you want to wear them? Then wear them! You know, there's something especially exciting about someone who doesn't follow the trends, someone who follows their own interests and desires. If you really believe in it, do it. It may be one of the most exciting things about you!

Chapter 24

BIG MISTAKE #6

How many times have you heard people complain? I mean complain about anything. About a hundred times a day? Maybe five hundred times a day? And what are they complaining about. Everything under the sun - their job, their health, their car, their boyfriend, their girlfriend, their toe nails, the President...anything and everything! They obviously don't know that nobody cares. Everyone has problems of their own. They don't need other people's problems, too.

It gets worse, though. People keep the complaining up on a date. The ones who are really "dense" complain about the date itself!!! They may complain about the restaurant you're at, or the movie you went to (although you'd better not be going to dinner and a movie on a first date, remember?), or your car or the way you dressed. Sometimes, I think some people are from Jupiter. People on Earth must know better than to complain like this.

Complaining is one of the most unattractive things a person can do. We don't want to hear complaints. We want to hear about action. We want to hear about how a person is taking hold of what's wrong and making it right. And we don't want to hear complaints about a previous boyfriend or girlfriend, especially on a first date. Yet there are people who insist on doing just that.

You're out with a guy for the first time. The conversation is light, but then all of a sudden he starts talking about his last girl friend. He tells you about how badly she treated him, how she had no respect for him, how she took advantage of him and on and on. You barely know the guy and he's drilling this girl into the ground. What's he going to be saying about you to the next person? Makes you wonder, doesn't it?

Another all too common complaint is "There just aren't any good men (or women) left". Boy, that's going to make me feel great if I'm on a date with this person. Here I am trying my best to keep some good conversation going, planning some fun things to do and all in all making everything go as right as I can. Then, the girl I'm with hits me with that line - "There just aren't any good men left.". What am I, a pile of kidney beans? Now, you might be laughing because you just don't believe someone would be dumb enough to say that on a date. Or, you're laughing because you remember it happened to you!

Sometimes the complaints seem endless. You thought you were out on a date with someone who liked having a good time, was popular and friendly. Then they come out with "You know, I haven't had a date in 6 months. It's been terrible!". There's another great complaint for you. The first thing I'm going to wonder about is what's wrong with this person that she hasn't been out in six months. I know that sooner or later I'll find out what it is. I just hope I find out sooner!

Keep the complaints to yourself. As I said at the beginning of this chapter, no one is interested. Complaining is boring and annoying. People want to hear about your good times, your successes, your action. They don't want to hear the list of 75 reasons you hate your boss.

Chapter 25

BIG MISTAKE #7

Throughout this book I have mentioned bars and dating services. Remember, I'm not totally against them. I'm not totally in favor of them either. Thus, the next big mistake.

Some people depend on dating services and bars for a good portion (or even all) of their social lives.

A BIG MISTAKE!

I've probably mentioned it before, but you should always go with the numbers. Not only in dating, but in life. If you are looking for a job, you don't just send out one resume, do you? (You do???). Go with the numbers. The more strings you have in the pond, the greater the chance of getting a fish.

LIFE'S A NUMBERS GAME.

The bars are just packed with people every Friday night. So, you say, that should be a good example of going with the numbers. Well, in a way you are right. There are lots of people, so there is a greater chance of meeting someone. Sounds logical, but it's not.

The major problem with the bars is that they are a very artificial atmosphere and they make people act artifically. The people are often artificial; what they are saying is artificial, the way they are acting is artificial. It's no wonder that people are amazed at what a person is like outside the bar atmosphere. You didn't see the real person in the bar. So, why are you amazed that the person is different outside of the bar?

Another major problem with the bars is that they can be very ego-damaging. Now, let's face it, not many people go to bars to meet their friends and talk. Many people go hoping to meet Mr. or Miss America. They go with expectations. Sometimes rather unrealistic expectations. When their expectations are not met, they are hurt.

While they're in the bar, they may say or do things that they did not particularly want to say or do. They may feel compromised. Not a real healthy feeling.

As for dating services -- they can be great. BUT, when people depend on them to be their <u>sole means</u> of meeting people, again, there's trouble. In the last several years, a number of "exclusive" dating services have surfaced. For outrageous fees, you are told that you will meet the "cream of the crop". Unfortunately, the reality is not always the same as the advertising.

I have spoken with lots of people about their experiences with dating services. Not one person has ever had a terrific success story to tell me.

Now, obviously, this is not a very scientific method of investigating dating services. But, this is how most people get information -- word of mouth.

In theory, dating services are a great idea. Lots of people join. You get to see photos or tapes or descriptions of the people available. You make your selection. The other person makes his or her selections and the matches are made.

Again, the reality is not always the same as the theory. The complaint I heard most often from people who used dating services is that they didn't feel they got what they paid for. They found very little of what they felt was the "cream of the crop". They found nice (and sometimes not so nice) people, but no one special. One woman I spoke to told me that she spent over $5,000 on a dating service membership. In one year she was matched with only one person -- and he couldn't even hold a conversation. So, not only was she out over $5,000 - she also felt very foolish for having done this in the first place.

Am I totally thumbs down on dating services? No. But I want you to use caution. I've seen dating services advertised for very reasonable prices. Some as little as $27 for a 3 month membership. For $27, I'd give it a try. Not much to lose and the possibility of a lot to gain. Try it. In fact, in just a minute I'll give you more information about this $27 dating service.

But $5,000? I personally think you would have to have your head examined to pay that much without also getting a fabulous, iron-clad guarantee...and I don't know of any such guarantee.

So, what's the bottom line here. Are dating services and bars completely out? No. Definitely not. But they should not be as high on people's lists as they are made out to be. They can be fun. They can be useful. But, they should only be one more line in the pond. You shouldn't give up complete control of your social life to a dating service or the people at a bar. Instead, you should be out doing what you love to do.

If you go out to a bar and find no one, what have you gotten out of the experience...smoke in your hair, a few drinks in your system and maybe a few attacks to your ego. But, what if you went to a charity benefit, or a concert, or a ball game or lots of other such things and you don't find someone of interest? Well, at least you've been entertained and have had a good time. Sounds like a deal to me!

OK, now to the information about the $27 dating service. The name of the service is Dateline. While I was writing this book, I actually joined this service. I didn't tell them who I was.

I WAS THRILLED WITH THE RESULTS!!!

The women I met were <u>very</u> desirable. I got guaranteed results for $27 - less than the cost of a cheap night out with <u>no</u> guarantees!

I'm so impressed with Dateline that I'm putting an application right in this book. If you'll turn to the very last page of this book, you'll find it. You can either photocopy it or tear it out. Then just fill it in and send it off. I want you to join. I'm sure you'll be pleased.

I also have another recommendation. If you <u>do</u> go to the bars, make the most of them. Bryan Redfield, a California bartender, has produced an audio cassette tape for women called "*A Bartender's Guide for Women: How to Meet Men*." He's also written a book for men called "*A Bartender's Guide on How to Pick-Up Women*." There's more information about both of these products on the next page. The information in each of them is superb.

If you're going to bars, get them...they'll put the odds <u>heavily</u> in your favor!!!

LEARN THE BEST WAY TO MEET MEMBERS OF THE OPPOSITE SEX

-- ASK A HOLLYWOOD BARTENDER WHO KNOWS --

Are you looking for someone to love? Would you like to know the BIGGEST MISTAKES people make - and how YOU can avoid them? Have you tried all of the great opening lines and found out all they did was to make you look foolish? Would you like to know why? Do you want to know the FIRST THING a good prospect REALLY notices about someone they're attracted to, and the MOST EFFECTIVE way to get the attention of someone you are interested in? Want to be able to separate the good prospects from the bad, in thirty seconds or less? Would you like to learn the BEST WAY to meet, and ask out, the person of YOUR CHOICE using class, style, and dignity? Then let Bryan Redfield's FOURTEEN YEARS OF EXPERIENCE IN HOLLYWOOD'S HOTTEST NIGHTCLUBS work for YOU. He EXPLODES the myths and shows you what REALLY works. ANYONE can use these techniques, REGARDLESS OF YOUR AGE. And they CAN BE USED ANYWHERE, not just in a bar. It is EASY ONCE YOU KNOW HOW.

YOU WILL OUTCLASS YOUR COMPETITION AND GAIN AN UNFAIR ADVANTAGE
OVER THE DATING PROSPECTS YOU MEET BY LEARNING:

- what to wear, what not to wear - and why
- how to find the hottest bars in your part of town - FOR FREE
- how most guys ruin their chances with a woman before they even open their mouth - and how you can avoid that mistake
- how to tell if the other person really wants to meet you
- 39 Deadly Classic Mistakes you can avoid
- how to be yourself, how to be honest, and how to establish common ground
- Women - effective ways to handle a bad prospect
- Women - guaranteed ways to prevent date rape
- Women - how a good prospect feels about having a woman call him on the phone and ask him out for a date
- how to call someone on the phone and ask them out for a date
- Men - why buying her a drink is a big mistake
- Men - the 25 things a woman wants to know about you when she first meets you
- at what point in the relationship should you consider sex
- where to go on the first date - and why
- how to find out what kind of a dating prospect they are by asking them 3 simple questions

You will also get the results of over 200 single, attractive men and women who took the same survey. And you will find out what the results mean. Bryan has been interviewed by over fifty radio and three TV stations across America and Canada. You will find out why the women on ABC TV's KELLY & CO. in Detroit gave Bryan a standing ovation and then you will know why the PLAYBOY CHANNEL gave Bryan's book their HIGHEST RATING! THERE IS ABSOLUTELY NO OTHER INFORMATION LIKE THIS IN EXISTENCE THAT HAS BEEN WRITTEN BY A QUALIFIED AUTHORITY. We are SO CONVINCED you will LOVE this 345 page, 93,000 word, 19 chapter book - and our 90 minute audio cassette (for women only) - that we offer it to you with an UNCONDITIONAL 1 YEAR MONEY BACK GUARANTEE. If you are dissatisfied with it FOR ANY REASON simply return it for a FULL REFUND. We are THAT CONVINCED you will LOVE this material. Because he is a bartender, Bryan Redfield has access to information the other authors on this subject only dream about. So stop listening to amateurs and get the TRUTH from a professional. ORDER TODAY!!! Because no river is deep to the person that knows how to swim.

Book - A BARTENDER'S GUIDE ON HOW TO PICK UP WOMEN. (Ladies: Don't be fooled by the title. This book is packed with good, solid advice for women, too. As a matter of fact, we have found as many women buying this book as men because the material is so pro-women.)   Only $19.95 each plus $3.05 postage + handling.

90 Minute Audio Cassette - A BARTENDER'S GUIDE FOR WOMEN: HOW TO MEET MEN. (Sorry guys, this one is designed for women only.)   Only $19.95 each plus $3.05 postage + handling.

To order using VISA/MasterCard, call: 1-800-688-6283
Or, send check or money order to:
❖ **Ultimate Secrets**
PO Box 43033, Upper Montclair, NJ 07043

Chapter 26

BIG MISTAKE #8

People are <u>too open too soon</u>. They're not mysterious enough. They tip their hands at the beginning of the game. They don't hold any intrigue.

Have you ever been out with someone, either dating or just casually, who gave you their whole life story in about 20 minutes - sometimes 20 non-stop minutes? Well, then you know what I mean. Everything is exposed eary in the game. The good news and the bad. The successes and the therapy.

Don't get me wrong - I'm not advocating keeping secrets in a relationship. But I am suggesting that some intrigue should always be lingering.

As a relationship develops, important information should come out - it has to come out. Many times if certain information doesn't come out early, it can be damaging later.

But it's really exhausting to hear a person go through his or her entire life resume on a first or second meeting. Within minutes you know what languages this person speaks, you know all about their childhood, their schooling, their job history, their income (or lack of). You find out about their parents and their relationship. You find out what they're good at and what they're not - the mistakes they've made and the mistakes they never hope to make again.

DON'T GIVE TOO MUCH INFORMATION

Lighten up a bit. Everything has it's time. The first or second date is not the time to open the floodgates.

I find it very intriguing to go out with a woman to play raquetball and have her blow my doors off. Now, I'm a pretty fair raquetball player and not too many people can blow my doors off - male or female. And along comes this date who, without warning, runs up a score of 21-6. Or when we go out to dinner, she orders in French. Or I find out about some prestigious award she's gotten --

AND I DON'T FIND OUT FROM HER!

OK, you may be the kind of person who wants to hear information right from the source. That's fine. But I don't think there are too many people interested in hearing anyone rattle off a list of their accomplishments. When I hear this, I wonder why the person is doing this. Are they so insecure that they have to have their medals displayed immediately? Do they think I won't find them worthy unless they do this?

Now, when we're talking about information like "I'm separated from my wife (or husband)" or "I travel three weeks out of every month on business" or "I could never date anyone out of my religion", now we're talking about important information that should come up early.

But things like "I graduated summa cum laude from State University" may be something to hold back. I'd be much more impressed to see the diploma on the wall and read it there for the first time. How about you? I feel that not only is this person quite intelligent, but she also is not out to simply impress me with accomplishments.

We've all been told that people who constantly talk about themselves do so because they're insecure. I certainly believe it. Talking about the other person not only makes the other person feel good, it also keeps some mystery about you. Again, don't play the game of keeping secrets. But also, don't focus the spotlight on you. I've often wondered what happens when two people who know they should be talking about the other person, get together. How does their discussion go? Something like "Well, what do you do?" - "Oh, let's not talk about me. What do you do?" - "Oh, we can get to that later. What do you do?". And on and on forever. Probably not, but it's fun to think about it.

People love intrigue and mystery. Look at the books that sell the best. But just as much as they love intrigue and mystery, people hate having important information kept from them. Use this to your benefit. Have fun keeping people wondering what will come next. What can you do next? Let them be impressed by your talents as they come up. Don't try to impress them with a resume of talents up front. It usually becomes little more than a bore.

Chapter 27

BIG MISTAKE #9

Mistake #9? Not being enthusiastic enough...or, being <u>too</u> enthusiastic. Now, before you think we have just a narrow range of enthusiasm to fall into, let me explain.

Remember back in high school when you had a subject you didn't think you would especially enjoy -- maybe science, or English or math. You walked into that class with a predetermined attitude -- "I'm not going to like this class, <u>no matter what</u>." Then the instructor started to talk about the class. She started to tell stories about what you would learn, how exciting it would be, how you would be able to use it every day of your life - maybe to make money - maybe to make friends. However you used it, it was going to give you great rewards. Things you really wanted.

I'm not talking about the typical propaganda you got from teachers. I'm talking about the truth that came from the teacher's heart. You knew it was true because you could see the genuine sense of enthusiasm she had for the subject. Her eyes lit up when she talked. She had a big, genuine smile when she told you about the subject. She was so enthusiastic it made you start to wonder. Could history actually be exciting? After all, look at how enthusiastic that teacher is standing up there telling you how exciting it is.

So, you start to check it out. Her enthusiasm has gotten you. She's made her subject exciting because she was enthusiastic about it. So, you became interested. It's a direct relationship! Enthusiasm causes excitement. Enthusiasm is very attractive.

On the opposite end of the spectrum, there are people who can make winning the lottery sound downright boring.

IT ALL DEPENDS ON THE PERSON'S LEVEL OF ENTHUSIASM

This also holds true on a date or even on simply meeting someone of the opposite sex.

You may not have the world's most glamorous job, but if you're enthusiastic about it, you'll capture the other person's interest and imagination. They'll have that same feeling you had when you were in school. You'll mention that you're a security guard, or an accountant or whatever. The other person will probably have preconceived ideas about the job. They might not think the job is exciting. But then, you describe some of the things you do, with genuine enthusiasm.

You talk about how someone was breaking in in the middle of the night. How it was dark and quiet. How you were the only person there. The only person who knew about the break-in. You talk about how you very quietly crawled behind the desks and counters, following the person until you got to the light switch, flipped it on and yelled "Keep your hands in the air & don't turn around." How you didn't even have a gun, but faked it while you called the police. How you single-handedly prevented the theft of millions of dollars worth of rare gems. You very easily draw the other person into the excitement because of your enthusiasm.

The opposite can also be true. You might be an astronaut scheduled to fly on the next shuttle mission. But, if you talk about how early you're going to have to get up to get to the launch pad, how you're probably going to get motion sickness when you're in orbit, how there's absolutely no privacy in the bathroom on the shuttle, and so forth, you'll have the other person bored in seconds.

This holds true not only in talking about your job, but also in talking about your life. Did you know that there are over 1600 things that can go wrong with a person's body? That's 1600 diseases, discomforts, problems and difficulties that can affect the human body. Have you ever met people that seemed to have experienced all 1600...and wanted to tell you about every single one of them? I don't care how enthusiastic you get, no one is going to become entranced by your description of how the pain in your lower back slowly spreads down your leg.

Each and every one of us has an interesting life. The problem has to do with whether or not we believe we have an interesting life. If we don't feel that we are interesting and have interesting lives, that's what we convey. If, on the other hand, we are convinced that we are interesting characters with interesting things to say, that's what the world sees. We get to decide exactly what the world's view of us will be. What an opportunity!

When I started this chapter, I mentioned that mistake #9 was actually two mistakes in one. Namely, not being enthusiastic enough and being too enthusiastic. This second part, being too enthusiastic, is just as deadly as the first.

You've met people who are too enthusiastic. You know what I mean. They seem to gush about everything. They talk in superlatives all the time.

Everything is "incredible", "wild", "the greatest". The superlatives never end. When you encounter these people, you often back off..literally.

Some people call them "Sparkle Farkles". People that beam the ear to ear smile every minute of the day. People who have the cute little phrases and sayings for everything -- "If someone doesn't have a smile, give them yours." You know. The stuff you see in greeting cards and on posters. It's not the stuff that people really say in everyday conversation. This is too much enthusiasm. It's phony. It's not the way people really feel. The smile is not genuine; it's put on. The sayings are memorized; they're not from the heart. Their over-bubbly personality wears you out. Actually, you're probably being worn out just reading about them.

Enthusiasm is one of the most endearing qualities a person can have, when it's genuine...when it comes from the heart. It draws people in. It creates excitement. It adds energy. It's just plain fun. When you honestly feel enthusiasm for something, it shows. People know it...and they appreciate it. It'll win you more members of the opposite sex than just about anything else you can do. Use it to it's maximum advantage.

GET YOUR "MOST WANTED" LOVER NOW

THE SECRET GUIDE
TO GETTING ANY LOVER YOU WANT *EASILY*

IT TAKES ONLY A FEW HOURS TO MASTER,
BUT YOU'LL USE IT FOR THE REST OF YOUR LIFE!

Don't let yourself suffer needlessly from loneliness. Always remember: You deserve only the best for yourself, and I won't let you settle for anything less. That's why I'm making these secret methods available at this time. They've worked for the F.B.I., and they'll work for you! But you have to take the first step.

If you keep talking about wanting a great love life, but just can't seem to make it happen, then STOP EVERYTHING until you get this book! It can EASILY and absolutely change your life if you're lonely or even just bored. And it will greatly improve your current relationships.

Now what's to stop you from ordering right this minute?

1. THE MONEY? It costs no more than a decent T-shirt or one real cheap night out. This can't be the reason!

2. THE GUARANTEE? If at any time EVER, you decide this book is not worth many, many times it's small cost to you...just return it in resalable condition for a complete refund. No questions asked! The risk is all mine. The benefits are all yours.

3. NOT SURE IF IT WILL REALLY WORK FOR YOU? Just get this book in your hands, take a few hours to read it, study it, even try out some of the methods you'll learn. It will absolutely put your love life on automatic cruise. That's how confident I am that you will get your MOST WANTED LOVER...the one you deserve to have!

4. DON'T HAVE THE DESIRE TO CLIMB OUT OF THE BACK SEAT AND FINALLY GET BEHIND THE STEERING WHEEL? It's time to stop letting everybody else drive you around in life. By ordering this very moment, you are finally taking control of your own love life. YOU will never again tolerate anything but the very, very best for yourself. And you'll get it!

NOW! Send $22.95, postpaid, to
ULTIMATE SECRETS
Box 43033
Upper Montclair, NJ 07043

TO CHARGE YOUR PURCHASE TO YOUR
VISA OR MASTERCARD
CALL 1-800-688-MATE

DO YOURSELF A FAVOR THAT WILL LAST A LIFETIME

Chapter 28

BIG MISTAKE #10

The last of the "10 Biggest Dating Mistakes You Can Make" is the biggest of them all.

IT'S BIGGER THAN THE OTHER NINE PUT TOGETHER

It's the one that's responsible for more unhappiness in dating and in relationships than anything else.

The 10th mistake, very simply, is that people don't "go for it". From beginning to end, they don't go for it. They don't go for the people that interest and excite them. Instead they settle for the people that are easy for them to approach or people who virtually throw themselves at someone.

They don't say what they want to say. They don't do what they want to do. They don't look for the person that absolutely thrills them and then try for him or her.

They don't try a variety of approaches to meet people.

They don't try a variety of people, a variety of places, a variety of techniques.

Again, this can pertain to people's entire lives, not just their dating lives. Most people have wonderful dreams. They dream of who they want, what they want. Their dreams excite them. Sadly, they remain dreams. Too rarely do they turn into realities.

Why?

If you have been paying attention to what you have read, you already know the answer.

Right. It's fear.

People are afraid of what will happen to them if they go after what they want -- that special man or special woman, for instance. Would you believe that people are also afraid of what will happen if they <u>do</u> get what they want? What will happen if they do get that date with the gorgeous man or woman -- will it last? Will people look and wonder how they got that man or woman to go out with them? Will they continually have to impress the other person to keep them? Will their dream actually turn into a living hell?

If I were able to banish anything from the face of the earth, it wouldn't be cancer or AIDS or nuclear weapons. It would be fear. Without fear, almost every one of our problems would disappear on its own. We wouldn't have to do anything else. The problems would be gone.

I'll even bet that you could do just about everything wrong in your approach to the opposite sex, but if you had no fear, you would <u>still</u> be successful. You could say the wrong words, wear the wrong clothes, approach people that would appear to be "out of your league". If you had no fear, you would be surrounded with delightful members of the opposite sex for the rest of your life!

That's all it takes -- letting go of that fear. Have you ever tried it? No? Why not? What? You're afraid!!! Hmmmmm.

We all go through highs and lows in our feelings of confidence. One day, when you are at one of those highs, be daring. Go talk to as many members of the opposite sex as you can. Don't even ask them for a date. Just talk to them.

A friend and I are very competitive. We make up contests just so we can compete. Once we had a contest to see who could ask the greatest number of women for their names. That's it. All we wanted was their name. This wasn't some great pick-up scheme. Just a silly contest we devised.

I won the contest by asking over 230 women their names in 30 minutes. After it was all over, we looked back at what we had done. We talked about how the women responded. It dawned on us that lots of these women had big smiles on their faces when they gave us their names. What did the smiles mean? Very simply, they meant "My name is Chris and you can talk to me if you'd like. I won't bite your head off." We realized that from a silly little game like this, we could have wound up with dates for months!

Nest time you're at a high point in your confidence cycle, talk to more of them...more men or more women.

The third time you're on this high, talk to them again, but this time ask one or two out. Or, if you can't talk to them yet, place a personal ad and mail it or call it in to the paper before your confidence starts to slip away. That way you've committed yourself.

Does all of this sound a bit crazy to you? I'm sure it does. It seems so easy. You want a date? Go talk to someone you are attracted to and get a date! Simple.

Apparently, it's not that simple. That's the real value of this book. That's why there are many other books on the same subject. It's that old devil: fear.

As for the few final words in this chapter, I want to again remind you of all you could have in this life if you're able to put fear aside. Fear is not something you were born with.

You made up the fear.

Read those two paragraphs over and over until you believe them in your heart. Aside from the normal self-protecting fears, fear is not something you were born with. You made it all up.

Now, stop making up fear. Belive in confidence.

Believe in <u>yourself</u>!

PEARL & NATURAL
天然的珍珠
The Oriental Secret To Healthier, Younger-Looking Skin.

SECTION 3

THE SECRETS

Chapter 29

THE GREATEST PICK-UP LINE OF ALL TIME

"You can't judge a book by its cover."

You've heard it. WELL, IT'S WRONG! And when it comes to meeting people of the opposite sex, this quote is worse than wrong...

IT'S DANGEROUS!

Because you do judge a book by its cover. So does everyone else in the world. We do judge people by initial appearances. We're attracted <u>and</u> repelled by first glances.

What usually happens is that when you meet a new person, you spend the first 30 seconds judging. So, the first 30 seconds is the make-it-or-break-it time.

"Do I like him/her or not???"

Then, and get this, you spend the rest of the time confirming your original judgment.

So, the initial impression gives us the answer to the question "Do I like him or her?"

And the rest of the time, the person searches for reasons why they like or dislike this person.

But wait...fear not...you're going to learn exactly what you have to do to make the best impression possible so you can win them over each and every time.

There's help right in your hands. In this chapter you're going to learn...

THE GREATEST PICK-UP LINE OF ALL TIME...

The one best way to meet that person of your dreams...or anyone else, for that matter.

Let's get to that pick-up line right now. We'll start with some nominations for the greatest pick-up line of all time.

The envelope please...

1. "You come her often?"

2. "Haven't we met before?"

3. "Didn't you go to State College?"

Now, these are pretty awful, right? They're bad, but none of these innane openings are committing.

The most devastating error you can make in a social situation is to say nothing.

Believe it or not, in meeting the opposite sex, saying something will always - yes, always - work better than saying nothing.

You've been in that situation yourself. You see that ideal person across the room and you say nothing - zero, zip. How far did you get with that person? Right, nowhere. You got absolutely nothing out of that situation.

If you said anything at all, you couldn't have wound up with less! You didn't say anything and you wound up with nothing. If you said anything at all and still wound up with nothing, you're right back where you started. No loss. There isn't anything less than nothing!!!

Remember this rule:

NOTHING WILL HAPPEN UNTIL YOU SAY SOMETHING

So, now you're ready for the greatest pick-up line of all time...

I'm going to make it really simple.

I'm going to give it to you in one word.

The greatest pick-up line of all time is...

ANYTHING!

Don't give me that look! Don't roll your eyes! It's true. Saying anything will always work better than saying nothing. Do you get tongue-tied because you feel that you're being evaluated by that other person? Well, you're right, you are. Welcome to the club.

But, isn't it better to be evaluated than not having that person know you exist? So, don't worry so much about what you say and how you sound -- just say something...anything.

Here are my 3 rules for saying anything:

Rule #1. Ask a question -- don't make a statement. As every great sales person in the world knows (and you are a "social salesperson" in this case --you're selling yourself) questions get the listener involved.

Rule #2. Never ask a closed-ended question. Always ask open-ended queries. A closed-ended question can be answered with a "yes" or "no". Watch the great talk show hosts like Larry King, Oprah Winfrey, Phil Donahue. They ask open-ended or "involving" questions. When a person says "yes" or "no" the conversation is stalled. Open-ended questions begin with the words "who", "what", "where", "when", "why" & "how".

Rule #3. Talk about the other person. Don't talk about you. Basically, you are asking them about themselves in a very easy going way. (WARNING: DO NOT INTERROGATE THEM.)

If you talk about the other person, here's what will happen. First, they'll know the answers. Second, they'll be doing most of the talking (so you won't have to worry about how nervous you're feeling and what you'll say next). And third, if they're the one doing the talking, they'll be fascinated. Nobody is bored when they're talking about their all-time favorite subject -- themselves. So, after your initial conversation, they'll think you are indeed very interesting!

So, the magic pick-up line is simply to say anything!!

And once again, this great "secret" works equally well for men and women.

Remember, you're not going to be universally loved and accepted. But, you can maximize your chances of finding the love of your life by remembering these three things:

#1. Socially, your job is to meet the most eligible, appealing and compatible people in the world.

#2. You do this by realizing that you are in the people business. Everything revolves around meeting people and networking. So, you are in the numbers game. The more people you meet, the greater your chances of meeting the right people.

#3. See this not as a task but as the most enjoyable game in the world. See it for what it really is. The more passionate you are about playing this game, the more successful you'll be.

Chapter 30

THE GREATEST PLACE IN THE WORLD TO
MEET THE MAN OR WOMAN OF YOUR DREAMS

Bars are the greatest places in the world to meet the man or woman of your dreams...right?

No, bars are the <u>worst</u> places. Dances are the best places...

No, wait a minute. Dances are the worst places. The best place is at work....

Well, this discussion could go on forever. Bars <u>are</u> great for some people (despite what I've said). They're also disastrous for others. Some people thrive at dances. Others wilt. Everyone has their own opinion.

Here's the key, though.

These opinions are based on their own experiences, not on any "scientific evidence". I've met people (and probably so have you) who rave about bars. They think they are, without a doubt, the greatest places in the world to meet that perfect person. Other people shudder at the thought.

Lots of people have told me that they love going to singles dances. Not only do you get to dance, you just might meet someone terrific there. Now, I've got to say, that's a good attitude, which, in itself, is a good start. But these feelings are based on the actual experiences people have had at these places. They do well in bars or at dances. I think I can safely say that most people don't. They don't enjoy the "atmosphere" in bars. They don't enjoy the competition at dances.

Opinions are based on experience. I've actually read books and articles that deal with the "best place to meet women" or "the best place to meet men" - like such a perfect place exists. Believe me, it doesn't.

I remember when I was a very impressionable teenager, I would hear people say things like "If you can't meet someone there, there must be something wrong with you." So, I'd go there. And I wouldn't meet anyone. Being young and impressionable, what would be my next thought? Right! There must be something wrong with me. It sure did take me a while to figure out that there was absolutely nothing wrong with me. But there was something very wrong with me in that place. It just was not the place for me. I didn't feel comfortable there. Therefore, I didn't do well. I couldn't be myself.

So, now that I gave you this whole story about there not being a perfect place to meet people, you want to know why I titled this chapter "The Greatest Place in the World to Meet the Man or Woman of Your Dreams"?

Is the light bulb going on?

Right. I got you again. The answer is <u>ANYWHERE</u>.

There is no one greatest place to meet men or women. I don't care what anyone says. The greatest place to meet that person of your dreams is where you meet them! Now, if this seems like double talk to you, think about it again.

What's the problem with telling people about the "best" place to meet the person of their dreams? Right, everyone starts to show up at that place and now you're back to being a small fish in a big pond. The same thing happens with restaurants. One person discovers a great one. He tells his friend, who tells a friend, who tells a reviewer and there goes the secret.

So, even if there was a "greatest place in the world to meet people", it wouldn't be there for long. Soon, people would find out about it and it would be mobbed. Then, it wouldn't be the greatest place in the world to meet people anymore. Say, that's pretty philosophical, isn't it? Now, here I am, back to telling you that the greatest place to meet the person of your dreams is where you meet them. This isn't just a run around. It's the truth.

How often have you or a friend made a judgment based on what someone else told you? If you believe enough in what the person told you, it becomes the truth - whether or not it really is the truth. The movie becomes boring - the car becomes too flashy - you become sick when you were feeling fine just a few minutes earlier. That one's the best. You feel fine. Someone asks if you are feeling ill. You say no and ask why. They tell you you look terrible. You start to feel terrible.

So it is with places you meet other people. Friends tell you that the place you are going to is full of losers. You start to see nothing but losers.

The key here is to disregard the good opinions of others and venture out for yourself. Be open and available to meet new people wherever they are.

A funeral is certainly a sad and solemn occasion. Does that mean it is impossible to meet someone there? If you totally close your mind to the idea, the answer is yes; yes it's impossible to meet someone at a funeral. If your mind is <u>always</u> open to the possibility, you never know where you are going to meet someone. Now, don't go around telling people that I told you that funerals were great places to pick up men and women!!!

How about another true-to-life example. A friend of mine had volunteered to be auctioned off at a charity "date" auction. Men were going to bid on getting a date with women, my friend being one of them. Women were also going to be bidding on dates with men. My friend was afraid that no one was going to bid on her. So she asked me to come to bid on her. Here's that self-image problem again. She's beautiful. I knew very well that lots of men would bid on her, but I went anyway to give her moral support.

She was going to be the last person to be auctioned off. (That sounds terrible, doesn't it. Actually, it's lots of fun.) I was violating one of my own rules. I hadn't turned myself off to the idea of meeting anyone here. But, it wasn't on the top of the list of my thoughts. I had lots of other things on my mind and frankly this wasn't one of them.

I went with another male friend. We were talking about business and lots of other ideas when the auction started. We really weren't paying all that much attention to what was going on. Out strolls the first person to be auctioned - a stunning blond woman in a dazzling blue dress. All of a sudden my mind switched from business to "business". I realized that I had wandered off the track of clear thinking.

The auctioneer asked for an opening bid. NO ONE BID!!!! Why? They were all intimidated! The men were just staring at this woman. The auctioneer called out "How about a bid of $75?". Keeping in mind one of my favorite sayings "You snooze, you lose", I bid the $75. The auctioneer asked for $100. There was a long pause. A very timid hand rose from behind me and bid $100. I quickly shot up my hand, offering a bid of $125. The rest of the room sat paralyzed in what I guess was fear. I "bought" her for $125.

I can't resist telling people about great bargains I get. So, I've got to tell you about this one. Not only did I win this magnificent woman, she came with a date package. The package consisted of a day long canoe trip through a marvelous part of New Jersey (no wise guy, that's not a contradiction in terms), a picnic lunch and dinner for two at a gorgeous restaurant. To top it off, the money I spent went directly to a very worthwhile charity. Once again, a winning situation for all concerned.

Oh, you want to know what happened after the first date? There were dozens more. Quite a great adventure. And by the way, after I won my date, the rest of the people in the room started to loosen up. Each person who followed her brought more and more money. My friend, who was the last person to be auctioned off, brought $1,100! So, not only did I get the biggest bargain of the night, I also got the best woman, if I do say so myself.

You never know when or where you are going to meet someone intriguing, attractive and irresistible. If you close your mind to any possibilities, you may be cutting yourself off from the very people you've been longing for for your entire life.

I'm still going to stand firm on what I've said about bars, dating services, singles dances and the like. Don't rule them out of your agenda. Just don't spend a great deal of your effort there. Remember, you become that little minnow in a big lake. Instead, you want to be a big fish in a little pond.

Chapter 31

THE BEST JOBS TO HAVE IF YOU
WANT TO MEET FABULOUS PEOPLE

If you've read through this entire book and you still aren't sure where to meet that person you've been dreaming of, stay with me. In this chapter I'll be talking about the jobs you should get if you want to meet fabulous people. In fact, as most people will tell you, there's a list of five jobs that are somewhat famous for attracting the opposite sex. These are jobs that just about anyone can...

What's that? You don't believe me?

You don't think there is any such list of five perfect jobs for meeting people.

You think this is just another trick like the last two chapters?

You think I'm going to say that <u>any</u> job is a great job if you are looking to meet great people?

Well......

<u>CONGRATULATIONS!!!</u>

You've just graduated from *How to Be Outrageously Successful With the Opposite Sex* University. You've gotten the big picture! You're well on your way to truly Outrageous Success!

Of course there can't be any list of great jobs. The great people are where you find them. Once you start to narrow down the list to a few "chosen professions", you've seriously cut your chances for success.

If you've made a list of the professions you'd like your future mate to be, you're heading for disaster. I don't mean that the person you find may be a disaster (although that may be true, too). I mean that your chances for success have been cut dramatically.

I'm not real sure how the mechanics of this selective process work. Do people look at someone, find them appealing and go up to them and say

"Excuse me, are you a dentist? No? Sorry.". Why would anyone make a list of "desired occupations" anyway. It would seem that they aren't interested in dating a person, they want to date a job.

One of the major mistakes that people make in dating is reducing their options - and, thereby, reduce their opportunities. Some of the limiting factors include height, age, job, hometown, even things like hair color and eye color!!! These people have got to be in a fog. Can you image the chances a person would have if they are only interested in dating a blond, 6' 2" Swedish carpenter with green eyes...who lives only two minutes away! Don't laugh. Some people do just that. Then they wonder why they have those lonely Saturday nights.

Not for one second am I suggesting that you should compromise yourself. If there are certain qualities that you just have to have, fine. Look for them. But every once in a while, review your list of demands. Are you having success? Does the list seem reasonable? Is there something on the list that could be cut and not cause a problem?

Of course, there is the other side of the story. The person who would date anyone. They don't really care what the person is like. They just want a person.

So, there's that whole area in between. There are some things that really turn you on - I absolutely love women who are very intelligent with a lust for adventure, a love of life and a passion for excellence (in addition to being strikingly attractive and a non-smoker). Her hair color? I don't care. Her eye color, height, job, religion...I just don't care. The qualities I love I love with a passion. I don't want to dilute them with a demand for blue eyes, brown hair or Protestant.

What do I have to say about dating someone at work. You probably can guess. I'm entirely self-employed. But, if a were in the workforce (and I have been) and I met someone that drew me like a nail to a giant electromagnet, you'd better believe I'd go for it. I'd sure keep in mind the possibility of a problem if the relationship didn't survive. But I'd be darned sure that the relationship was run in a way that if it should end, there really would be very few, if any, problems.

The major cause for job related relatonship problems is the way the relationship is run. If relationships are run like lives are supposed to be run, these problems wouldn't exist. If people just keep respect and honesty in mind, even if a relationship should end, the problems are minimal. I'm not saying there isn't sadness and possibly regret. But they don't become the type of situations that cause office fury.

I remember watching a TV show years ago - I think it was the Mary Tyler Moore show. She was dating quite a dazzling man and obviously having a great time. Then came the end. With warmth and kindness, the man called an end to the relatonship. No lies. No devious maneuvers. No avoidance until the relationship dies. Just the plain simple truth. She wasn't happy, but she had great respect for the way he handled the situation. No problems.

This brings us right back to one of the bottom line theories of Outrageous Success With the Opposite Sex. If you're straight-forward, go for what you want and don't put up all of those imaginary barriers in front of you, success just has to be yours. Not all of the time. But far more often than if you don't do these things.

I once heard someone say "If everyone in the world would just do what he or she is <u>supposed</u> to do, there would never again be any problems in the world." Of course that's very altruistic, but it's true. At least it gives us something to shoot for.

The same can be said for relationships. If everyone would do what he or she is supposed to do, there would be no more problems in relationships. Unfortuantely, far too many people think that this is a great rule...for the other person.

Chapter 32

ONE OF THE MOST IMPORTANT PHONE NUMBERS YOU'LL EVER HAVE

We're headed toward the end of our trip together, so it's time for me to get my closing thoughts together and to give you your final peptalk.

One of the biggest problems we all have to cope with is keeping up motivation. When you keep your motivation in high gear, you've got half of any problem licked. But, sometimes keeping at a peak is a problem. Don't be concerned. It's only human. We all go through the ups and downs. But, as the saying goes, it's not how many times you're knocked down that makes you a winner, it's how many times you get back up.

Hopefully, you have a good friend nearby - either in person or by phone. Someone who shares your dreams and understands where you are going. If you have such a person, you are truly fortunate.

For me, that trusted person has been Dr. Rob Gilbert. A good friend for over 10 years, Dr. Gilbert is always there with encouraging words, ingenious ideas, great anecdotes and a real jolt of energy when it's needed.

What's that you say? You don't have a Dr. Gilbert nearby? Oh yes you do. Dr. Glbert is a specialist in sport psychology. He's also at the top of the list of motivational speakers. In fact, here's a blatant plug for Rob. If you are looking for a dynamic, energetic, entertaining speaker for your sales meeting, convention or other group meeting, call him at

(201) 743-4428

Talk to him about what he can do for you. I guarantee it's plenty. He also does private coaching and consulting. I've seen the results. They are absolutely amazing.

OK. So you say that you don't want private coaching and you don't need a speaker for a meeting. You can still take advantage of Dr. Gilbert's expertise - and for FREE!

Dr. Gilbert offers a terrific, free service called "Peptalk". It's a 3 minute recorded motivational message. The messages are changed every week. There's no charge for the service, except for any charge your phone company makes for the call. These messages will instantly charge you with a bolt of energy. You'll get off the phone with a new enthusiasm. Without a doubt, it will be the best 3 minutes of your day.

The phone number for Peptalk is:
(201) 743-4690.

You can call anytime of the day, 365 days a year. You can also call as often as you want.

I've given you the answers to the problem. I've also given you lots of motivation. But sometimes there just isn't enough motivation in a book. You need the spoken word. Peptalk will give it to you.

And while we're on the subject, I know that there must be other services, similar to the Peptalk idea, available. If you know of any such services, please let me know. I'll check them out and, if they are published in the next edition of *How to Be Outrageously Successful With the Opposite Sex*, I'll give you credit and send you a free copy.

Keeping your motivation up is a key ingredient to success. Work on it and use Peptalk to help you.

Chapter 33

THE END OF THE ROAD

My friend, we've come to the end of our journey together. But it's been a ball. We've had lots of laughs together. We explored a subject that's been discussed since the beginning of time. But we looked at it in a different way. A way that's never been considered before. A way that has a great chance for dazzling success. In fact, a way that virtually guarantees success - for anyone.

We started out by talking about the problem. We talked about what it is, why it exists, what you want to do about it.

Then we looked at ways of solving the problem. Ingenious ways - lots of them.

Your imagination was teased. Your heart was made to beat a little faster. Your dreams came a little closer.

What you read in this book is real. It's exciting. It can be yours. All you have to do is take it.

In fact, one of the great morals pointed out by this book is that <u>anything you want can be yours</u>. You just have to go for it. It's out there waiting for you.

Oh sure, sometimes you'll be teased a little bit. But that's just to make the game a little more interesting. The reward a little more valued.

Throughout my life I've gotten just about everything I've wanted. Is that because I have some special talents or abilities? Certainly not. In fact, when we meet you'll see for yourself. The only thing I have that (unfortunately) most people don't have is that belief that anything I want really <u>is</u> there for me to take. So I take it.

Life isn't anywhere nearly as difficult as most people make it. In fact, if life were a living being I'm sure that it would be scratching its head wondering why so many people are making things so hard for themselves.

Some people seem to have a misplaced passion for putting barriers in their own way. They take real joy in suffering through the trials and tribulations in life. Each little bump in the road becomes a scar and a new medal of honor to be proud of.

I don't know about you, but my feeling is that as long as my heart is beating I have no problems. When that heart stops, then I have a problem. But not before then.

When I speak before various groups its almost inevitable that someone (or several someones) will come up to me and say "But you don't know the problems I have." My answer to them is always the same. If your heart is beating you have no problems.

Now I don't mean for one second to make light of problems. Cancer and AIDS are very serious problems. Tornadoes and earthquakes cause devasation. Poverty and hunger are among the world's most serious problems. But still, in my mind, nothing is more serious than death. Let's put everything in perspective.

I can tell you that although I've had hundreds of people come up to me and tell me about their "problems", not one of them has been even close to being called serious. There wasn't one of those "problems" that I wouldn't gladly take if the alternative was death. Perspective. Perspective.

You have all the tools you need to achieve the success you want. You've defined what "Outrageous Success With the Opposite Sex" means to you. So, that gives you a goal. You have the tools to reach your goal. You know the path that you must take to achieve success. And, you have the motivational help you need. But now...the most important part of the whole package...

YOU HAVE TO PUT IT TO WORK!

You have to go out and put all of this into action.

There are thousands...no, millions of <u>magnificent members of the opposite sex out there just waiting for you</u> - whether you're male or female. Put the excuses aside. Put the fears to rest. The rewards are absolutely incredible.

And they're all out there...

Just waiting...

For you!

I'll be doing a lot of travelling around the country talking about this book. I'll be meeting thousands of people. I hope you're one of them.

When we do meet, tell me about your success. Tell me about the great people you've met. Tell me about the experiences you've had...and are still having. Tell me about how you've changed your life.

But, fair warning. Don't tell me about your problems, because I'll know that your heart is beating...so you couldn't have any problems.

Carpe Diem.

Your Catalog of Books, Tapes and Special Reports

Here Are Your Tickets To A Sensational Love Life

On these pages, you'll find a list of some of the most exciting, powerful and effective books, tapes and special reports available to single men and women anywhere. All of these products are by Paul Hartunian, author of the book *How To Be OUTRAGEOUSLY Successful with the Opposite Sex*. They're designed to give your love life a tremendous boost...to dramatically increase the number of people you're dating...or to put the odds of meeting that person of your dreams heavily in your favor.

UNCONDITIONAL MONEY-BACK GUARANTEE

If you're not completely satisfied with anything you purchase from this catalog, return it for a full, immediate, no-questions-asked refund. You have absolutely no risk!

THE BOOK

❑ *How To Be OUTRAGEOUSLY Successful with the Opposite Sex* - This book is packed from cover to cover with exciting, new, easy-to-use, virtually no-fail techniques men and women can use to meet and date members of the opposite sex. This book explains - step by step - techniques that even the shyest people can use to meet and date more men or women than they probably ever dreamed possible! Don't waste another minute - or another dollar - in singles bars. Get this book and solve any dating problems you've had...forever. **$19.95 + $3 shipping**

THE AUDIO CASSETTE TAPES

❑ *How To Be OUTRAGEOUSLY Successful with the Opposite Sex* - Now, you can hear the book on tape! A one hour condensed version you can pop in your car stereo or walkman and enjoy over and over.

❑ *The 10 Biggest Dating Mistakes You Can Make* - So many people make one or more of these mistakes - then they wonder why they're having dating or relationship problems. Get this tape and be sure you are not a victim of these mistakes!

❑ *How to Find the Love of Your Life in 90 Days or Less* - A perfect compliment to the special report of the same name. This tape takes you further into the step-by-step program designed to do exactly what it claims...help you find the love of your life in 90 days or less!

The above tapes are priced at $14.95 + $1.50 (S&H) for each tape, any 2 tapes for $24.95 + $2.00 (S&H), or all three tapes for $29.95 + $2.00 (S&H).

THE SPECIAL REPORTS

Each special report consists of 5 pages of single spaced, tightly packed information that can help you take giant leaps toward a <u>great</u> love life - the kind that most people only dream of. Each special report gives you step-by-step instructions on how to handle some of the most common - and most frustrating - situations singles face.

These special reports are only $4 each or $10 for any 3, postpaid.

❑ **#1 - *How To Meet The Love of Your Life in 90 Days or Less*** - A step-by-step program that is <u>guaranteed</u> to help you do exactly what the title says. If you don't, you don't pay for this report.

❑ **#2 - *The Greatest Personal Ad Ever Written & How You Can Put It To Work for You*** - Eight carefully chosen words in the headline of this ad brought 99 responses within just days!!! The responses came from women who were virtually begging to meet the writer of the ad. This special report is written for men, but women can certainly learn a lot from it too!

❑ **#3 - *What To Do When It's Not Working Out*** - If you're dating someone now and it's just not working out, you need this special report. It tells you what to do...and what <u>not</u> to do.

❑ **#4 - *The Dating Nightmare: How To Overcome the Anxiety You Feel When You Meet That Special Someone*** - The title of this special report says it all. If you've ever had that feeling, read this special report.

❑ **#5 - *Great Ideas for Great Dates*** - Tired of the same old "dinner and a movie" date? Want some ideas for truly unforgettable dates? This special report is packed with ideas guaranteed to leave a lasting impression.

❑ **#6 - *Why Health Clubs Are The Worst Places To Meet People...And How You Can Make Them The Best Places for You*** - If you've hit stone walls when you try to meet people at health clubs, you're not alone. This report will teach you how to turn health clubs into an almost endless supply of dates for you.

❑ **#7 - *Why Flowers Don't Work: Gifts You Can Give That Will Really Make an Impact*** - You don't need a stack of $100 bills to afford gifts that will really make an impression. This special report will give you ideas that will guarantee that people remember you.

❑ **#8 - *The 5 Things You Have To Do To Impress That Special Someone*** - Follow this list and you've got it made. Skip over even one of these...and you're on your own!

❑ **#9 - *The Ultimate Secret To Finding A Rich Man To Marry*** - This special report teaches you step-by-step what you have to do to find and marry a rich man. If that's what you're looking for, this if for you.

❑ **#10 - *How To Be The Center of Attention at Any Party in Just Minutes*** - Why go to a party and feel awkward and uncomfortable? Why compete against everyone else at the party when you can be the center of attention? Read this special report and find out how...easily and quickly.

❏ **#11 - *How To Bounce Back When You've Been Dumped*** - It's over. The relationship has come to an end. You can mope around and wallow in the blues...or you can read this report and learn how to bounce back.

❏ **#12 - *How Not to Kill a Relationship on the First Date*** - The first date is the critical test period. The future of your entire relationship could rest on this one date. Discover the secrets to making the first date a smashing success...and the mistakes that could make it a disaster.

❏ **#13 - *How To Date Celebrities*** - Have you ever dreamed of dating a celebrity? Celebrities... like the men and women you read about in the newspapers, see on TV and watch in the movies? Now you can. This special report will tell you how.

❏ **#14 - *The Ultimate Secrets To Getting Almost Anyone To Fall in Love With YOU*** - Sounds too good to be true? Judge for yourself. Read this special report and see if it doesn't tell you how to do exactly what it claims. Remember, it's guaranteed or you don't pay for it!

❏ **#15 - *Cheap Dates*** - Dates don't have to cost a small fortune to be exciting. This report is loaded with great ideas for inexpensive dates that will be fun...and will be remembered.

❏ **#16 - *Secrets Therapists Never Tell You About How To Feel Great About Yourself*** - One of the biggest problems haunting people is poor self-image. Most people just don't feel good about themselves... and it shows. This just doesn't have to be. You'll find out why when you get this report.

❏ **#17 - *How To Make Sure They'll Never Forget You*** - Do you want to make a real impression with everyone you date? With this special report, you can't fail... guaranteed!

❏ **#18 - *Chinese Restaurants and 30 Other Improbable Places To Meet The Love of Your Life*** - If the 31 places on this list are not on your regular list, you're missing your part of the jackpot. Get this report and find out where you should be.

❏ **#19 - *How To Tell If Your Relationship Is Headed For Disaster*** - Do you know the warning signs of a relationship that's headed for a crash? If not, you could be wasting a lot of time and risking a lot of heartache. This simple 5 page report could help you avoid disaster.

❏ **#20 - *How To Date Someone You Work With*** - What if the man or woman of your dreams turns out to be someone you work with? This report will tell you exactly how to turn that sticky situation into a sheer delight!

THE VIDEO

❏ ***How To Be OUTRAGEOUSLY Successful with the Opposite Sex*** - Author Paul Hartunian is interviewed and reveals dozens of his incredible techniques that are virtually guaranteed to get men and women more dates than they ever dreamed possible. Many of the techniques on this video cannot be found in any of Paul's other books, tapes or special reports. **$19.95 + $3 (S&H).**

Catalog
SPECIAL PACKAGES

❏ *How To Be OUTRAGEOUSLY Successful with the Opposite Sex* - This package consists of the book, the video tape and the audio tape cassette. If you bought each of these separately, you would pay $54.85 plus $7.50 (S&H). But, when you buy this package, you only pay **$39.95 + $3 (S&H)**.

❏ *The SUPERSTAR SINGLE Package* - This package gives you everything offered in this catalog -- at a super discount price. If you are truly serious about skyrocketing your love life...finding the man or woman of your dreams...or to simply get lots more dates, this is the package for you. You'll get the book, the video tape, all three audio tape cassettes, plus every one of the 20 special reports. In addition, you'll get two extra bonuses -- first, you'll get the special cassette tape *How To Supercharge Your Love Life*. It'll be a real eye opener! You'll also get our private list of singles publications around the country. Each listing will have the name of the publication, the address, the cost of a sample copy and the subscription price. Use this list to find the publications in your area and then use the techniques you learn in the book, video and audio cassettes to hit a goldmine of new dates! If you were to buy everything in this package individually, you'd pay $164.75 plus $11.50 (S&H) - a total of $176.25. But when you buy the "Superstar Single" package, you pay only **$129.95 postpaid**. That means you save $46.30!!!

Remember, if you are not completely satisfied with anything you purchase, don't hesitate to return it for a full, immediate, no-questions-asked refund.

HOW TO ORDER

Simply choose the special reports and other products you would like, then call:

1-800-688-MATE
(1-800-688-6283)

...to charge your purchase on VISA or MasterCard.

Or, if you prefer, make a copy of the ORDER FORM on the next page, fill it in, and send it with your payment or credit card information to:

❖ **Ultimate Secrets**
Box 43033
Upper Montclair, NJ 07043

Your order will be rushed to you by first class mail.

(You can also just type or print the items you want with your name & address on a blank sheet of paper. Be sure to print clearly and to include your name and address. It would also be a good idea to include your phone number in case we need to contact you about your order.)

BOOK

❑ *How To Be OUTRAGEOUSLY Successful with the Opposite Sex* **$22.95**

AUDIO CASSETTE TAPES

❑ *How To Be OUTRAGEOUSLY Successful with the Opposite Sex* $16.45
❑ *The 10 Biggest Dating Mistakes You Can Make* $16.45
❑ *How to Find the Love of Your Life in 90 Days or Less* $16.45
❑ Any 2 cassette tapes **$26.95**
❑ All 3 cassette tapes **$31.95**

THE SPECIAL REPORTS

❑ #1 - *How To Meet The Love of Your Life in 90 Days or Less*
❑ #2 - *The Greatest Personal Ad Ever Written & How You Can Put It To Work for You*
❑ #3 - *What To Do When It's Not Working Out*
❑ #4 - *The Dating Nightmare: How To Overcome the Anxiety You Feel When You Meet That Special Someone*
❑ #5 - *Great Ideas for Great Dates*
❑ #6 - *Why Health Clubs Are The Worst Places To Meet People...And How You Can Make Them The Best Places for You*
❑ #7 - *Why Flowers Don't Work: Gifts You Can Give That Will Really Make an Impact*
❑ #8 - *The 5 Things You Have To Do To Impress That Special Someone*
❑ #9 - *The Ultimate Secret To Finding A Rich Man To Marry*
❑ #10 - *How To Be The Center of Attention at Any Party in Just Minutes*
❑ #11 - *How To Bounce Back When You've Been Dumped*
❑ #12 - *How Not to Kill a Relationship on the First Date*
❑ #13 - *How To Date Celebrities*
❑ #14 - *The Ultimate Secrets To Getting Almost Anyone To Fall in Love With YOU*
❑ #15 - *Cheap Dates*
❑ #16 - *Secrets Therapists Never Tell You About How To Feel Great About Yourself*
❑ #17 - *How To Make Sure They'll Never Forget You*
❑ #18 - *Chinese Restaurants and 30 Other Improbable Places To Meet The Love of Your Life*
❑ #19 - *How To Tell If Your Relationship Is Headed For Disaster*
❑ #20 - *How To Date Someone You Work With*

_____ **of the above special reports at** . . . . **$4 each**
_____ **groups of 3 of the above at** . . . . **$10 each group of 3**

VIDEO

❑ *How To Be OUTRAGEOUSLY Successful with the Opposite Sex* $22.95

SPECIAL PACKAGES

❑ *How To Be OUTRAGEOUSLY Successful with the Opposite Sex* - Book, Video, and Audio Cassette **$42.95**
❑ *The SUPERSTAR SINGLE Package* - Book, Video, 3 Audio Cassettes, 20 Special Reports, plus bonus tape and list **$129.95**

<<<<<<< All of the above prices include shipping & handling to U.S. >>>>>>>

PAUL, please send me the above checked items. I have enclosed payment in the form of...
❑ Check ❑ Money Order or ❑ Charge to my credit card (I have filled in my card information below):

VISA/MasterCard#:_____Exp. Date:_____

Signature:_____Phone:_____

SEND MY ORDER TO:

NAME:_____

ADDRESS:_____

CITY:_____STATE:_____ZIP:_____
Mail your order to: ❖ **Ultimate Secrets**, Box 43033, Upper Montclair, NJ 07043